Serious Fun

Homeschooling with Real Books

by

Kristin J. Draeger

Table of Contents

Preface to the Second Edition

I have produced a second edition so soon after the first for a couple of reasons. The first edition was rather hurried and unplanned, in preparation for a talk I gave at the local charter school. It sort of grew into a book by accident as I gathered together the stacks of materials I had used with my son over the years and listed them on my laptop sitting in front of the fire on Sunday afternoons during the weekly football games. As I rushed it to the printers I was aware that several sections were sparse at best, and when I received the first box of books (on the day of the meeting -- whew!) I became painfully aware that though I remembered to include a table of contents, I'd forgotten page numbers.

This edition remedies many of those problems. I have filled out some of the sparse sections (particularly modern history) and added over 400 titles in all. These include not only books, but games, puzzles, videos and music. I went back and listed new titles by authors who have continued to publish since my son and I enjoyed their work several years ago. I tightened up the format, fixed some glaring typos and, of course, remembered to add the page numbers. Although it could never be considered exhaustive (though it certainly has been exhausting) it is now, I hope, a more thorough and easy-to-use reference that will allow you to maximize and enjoy your homeschool time with your children.

Kristin J. Draeger
August 6, 2013

Introduction

Are you frustrated trying to teach school in a traditional way at home? Do your students have difficulty focusing and sitting still? Do you dread school time? Very early on I also became frustrated with homeschooling. I wanted homeschooling to be fun. I wanted to enjoy it. I didn't want it to be another thing like room-cleaning and teeth-brushing that I had to nag and force my child to do. This seemed wrong and antithetical to the whole idea of spending quality time together.

In addition, my son had some extra issues. He was not the type of 5-year-old who would sit at the table for 15 or 20 (or 5!) minutes at a time and print his abc's or write his numbers or even color a picture. Nor did he have any interest (or ability) in learning to read or write at an early age (He finally began reading at 8 and writing at 10 -- it turns out he was/is highly dyslexic). And all the time in the background homeschool gurus insist that literacy is primary and absolutely essential in these early years – everything depends upon it, they say.

On top of it all I was convalescing from a ten-year illness and teaching art history to 60 students per week so I didn't have a lot of time or energy to spend preparing creative lesson plans. So I was faced with a choice. We could fight our way through the early years with traditional curriculum and hope for a modicum of success (and hope our relationship survived it) or I could throw it all out the window and try something new.

So with much enthusiasm and a startling dose of fear I asked myself two questions: What did my son enjoy? And what was easy and enjoyable for me? The answer was books. Real books, not the dry, unimaginative textbooks that come with sets of curriculum, but fun books from the library or bookstore that were written to engage, inspire and entertain children. Though he wouldn't sit for workbooks, coloring books or sometimes even meals, my son would sit and listen me read 5 or 6 books in a row. So this is where I began.

Over the next few years I scoured the library and Amazon.com for kids' books that are both entertaining and educational, and what I found amazed me. I now have hundreds of fun books on science, history, literature, grammar and math (yes, math!). For the next four years (K-3rd) my son's education consisted mainly of reading books. Every day we would pull a science, history, literature, grammar and math book off the shelf and go sit down and I would read them to him. It felt like cheating. It felt wrong, but ultimately it felt great. We totally enjoyed it and we both looked forward to it (Yes, we did occasionally do some math and attempted reading, but it was sporadic. It was the exception, not the rule.).

The big question is, of course, did it work? And with a heavy sigh of relief I can say yes. Today he is in 9th grade and fits in just fine. He even gets high test scores and straight A's in his classes. I don't say this to brag, but to let you know that homeschooling can be done differently. It can be enjoyable and academic and easy.

The next question would then be, how did I do it? This is what a typical day looked like for my son and I when he was in the early (K-3rd) grades. At the beginning of our day I would pull a book from each of the subjects; that means I'd have a stack of six or seven picture books. Then we would go sit outside, or by the fire and read two or three books, take a break for a snack, laundry or errands and then read two or three more, take a break for more housework, and then finish the stack. While I did housework, cooked or prepared for the classes I taught, he might watch a *Magic School Bus*, or *Bill Nye the Science Guy* video (our day always included an educational video). I also tried to include a math game or geography puzzle. The skip-count math songs and science songs we kept in the car and would pop them in whenever we went somewhere. All-in-all, it was a bit haphazard, but it worked for us. Most importantly my son enjoyed the experience immensely. In fact, looking back he says that until he began the 4th grade he didn't know he was doing school at all.

This isn't to say that during kindergarten through third grade he never picked up a pencil. We did attempt some math worksheets and some printing, but not every day and not more than 10-15 minutes at a time. We did a lot of verbal math. He would jump on the bed and chant his addition tables, or bounce a ball or throw bean bags, anything that burned energy while we memorized.

Even as a five-year-old he began listening to chapter books. I would read about 30 minutes at a time and he would sit on the floor and put LEGOs together. Don't underestimate a child's ability to multi-task. My husband and I both at first doubted that he could truly listen and absorb the story AND build a flame-throwing, four-wheeled, turbo-boosted, whatcha-macallit, but he proved over and over that he could. At 5 I read

Mary Pope Osborne's *Odyssey* series and at 8 my husband read the *Lord of the Rings* trilogy to him (among many other titles). Many times we assumed that he was more engrossed in the LEGOs than the reading material, then we would come to a funny part in the story and he would burst out laughing, or ask a pertinent question at the right time. He was definitely paying attention.

By the time he was in the fourth grade I decided we should begin a math curriculum. At this point he could add and subtract, carry and borrow, and multiply two or three digit numbers, but that was all. He'd never done a full workbook or math text. In retrospect I would say if you could work four or five problems a day on paper from about 1st or 2nd grade on it would be ideal, but our experience was less organized.

Fourth grade marked a significant change in the way we organized our day. I wanted to keep reading the books that we loved, but we also had to add time for math and writing. At this point I joined with my sister and together we schooled my son and her two boys together. We divided the day into times and subjects and split the teaching of them between us.

Each day we spent 90 minutes doing math. The first 20-25 minutes I would read to them from one or more of the math books. The next 45 minutes they would work on their math curriculum and the final 20-25 minutes we would play a math game.

For the writing part of their day, fourth and fifth grades was almost exclusively journal writing. We depended on a book called *Unjournaling* by Cheryl Miler Thurston for writing prompts. The boys (10, 10 and 13) loved writing in their journals so they could read their entries to each other when they were finished. At this point the competition (often to see who could write the most bizarre, silly or gross entry) was essential. Why else would a 10-year-old boy write than to gross out his friends?

For grammar, my sister taught using the *Easy Grammar* series and would spend half the time reading grammar books to them and half the time working on the grammar worksheets.

A key element in his 4th-8th grade years was phonics tutoring. Though he was already becoming a proficient reader, at 10 my son couldn't write or spell at all and we had him tested for dyslexia and he scored rather high (high is bad, not good here). My sister's older son is also dyslexic and she began tutoring them both 30-60 minutes per day using Susan Barton's phonics program. Slowly over the next four years his writing and spelling improved nearly up to grade level.

During the 4th-8th grade years we still taught literature, science and history entirely by reading real books. At this point the boys still built LEGOs while we read, but they would also color maps, sit on those giant Pilate's balls (this is a must-have if you have boys), juggle, play with clay, yo-yo, or lie on the floor and stare into space. The only thing we required was silence.

All-in-all I was quite confident that using real books exclusively for literature, science and history wouldn't be a problem. I was more concerned about writing and math. As I said earlier, at 10 years of age my son couldn't write much more than his name and address with any confidence. In the fourth and fifth grades he began writing short journal entries. By sixth grade my sister had them doing short IEW (Institute for Excellence in Writing) lessons and in the seventh grade we practiced essays. In the eighth grade I signed him up with a local teacher who teaches homeschool literature/ writing classes out of her home and he began writing literature analysis essays on Shakespeare, Steinbeck and Hawthorne.The first semester of his eighth grade year he read 5 novels and finished 5 essays and received A's on all of them. My relief was palpable.

As far as math was concerned, in the fourth grade he began with Math-U-See's long division book. In the fifth grade we tackled fractions, in sixth grade percents and decimals, and seventh pre-algebra. In the eighth we began algebra and at the semester break he tried a local public charter school for the rest of eighth grade. I was nervous that he wouldn't be able to keep up in math with such a lean background, but he jumped into the algebra class and earned A's for the entire semester. All semester I waited for the other shoe to drop, so to speak, but it never did. After finals in May I finally let the breath out that I was holding and congratulated him on a great year.

He earned A's in all his other subjects as well, and I would like to report that he went on to high school and never looked back, but that was not the case. Though he was making amazing marks in his eighth grade public school experiment, he was not enjoying it. The school was a small local high school with a nurturing atmosphere. The teachers were kind and helpful and the student body was easy going. They boasted some of the highest test scores in the state, and called themselves a university-model school. Classes met twice a week and students we're responsible for homework on their off-days just like in college. But the core of the curriculum was textbooks and worksheets. He worked hard to get his A's, but he was bored. During the semester my husband and I saw his love of learning and his enthusiasm fall dramatically. So at the end of the year we pulled him out and this year we are back to homeschooling with more real books.

All this is to say that even during the later years, although math and writing need to be taught, it is still possible to rely heavily on real books. My son tolerated math and writing better as he got older, but still loved listening to and reading real books. The following is a list of books that I used and that I highly recommend. I have chosen only the best and have organized them in what, I hope, is an accessible way. They represent hundreds of hours of research on my part, and thousands of hours of writing and drawing on the part of the authors and illustrators whose works are represented here.

Enjoy.

Kristin J. Draeger

seriousfunk12.com
artk12.com
info@seriousfunk12.com

Online discussion of this book can be found at:

http://seriousfunk12.com/discuss

Real Math Books

Math Books for K-3rd Grades

General Math Books (K-3rd Grades)

- ☐ Allen, Nancy Kelly. *Once Upon a Dime: A Math Adventure.*
- ☐ Anno, Masaichiro. *Anno's Counting Book.*
- ☐ Anno, Masaichiro. *Anno's Counting House.*
- ☐ Anno, Masaichiro. *Anno's Magic Seeds.*
- ☐ Anno, Masaichiro. *Anno's Math Games.*
- ☐ Anno, Masaichiro. *Anno's Mysterious Multiplying Jar.*
- ☐ Birch, David. *The King's Chessboard.*
- ☐ D'Agnese, Joseph. *Blockhead: The Life of Fibonacci.*
- ☐ Demi. *One Grain Of Rice: A Mathematical Folktale.* Scholastic Press, 1997.
- ☐ Dodds, Dayle Ann. *Full House: An Invitation to Fractions.* Publishing, 2008.
- ☐ Duke, Kate. *One Guinea Pig is Not Enough.* Puffin, 2001.
- ☐ Duke, Kate. *Twenty is Too Many.* Dutton Juvenile, 2000.
- ☐ Einhorn, Edward. *Once Upon a Dime: A Math Adventure.* Charlesbridge Publishing, 1999.
- ☐ Einhorn, Edward. *A Very Improbable Story: A Math Adventure.*
- ☐ Ellis, Julie. *What's Your Angle, Pythagoras? A Math Adventure.*
- ☐ Ellis, Julie. *Pythagoras and the Ratios: A Math Adventure.*
- ☐ Fisher, Doris. *One Odd Day.* Sylvan Dell Publishing, 2007.
- ☐ Fisher, Doris. *My Even Day.* Sylvan Dell Publishing, 2007.
- ☐ Fisher, Doris. *My Half Day.* Sylvan Dell Publishing, 2008. Ghigna, Charles. *One Hundred Shoes: A Math Reader.*
- ☐ Gravett, Emily. *The Rabbit Problem.*
- ☐ Harris, Trudy. *Pattern Fish.*
- ☐ Harris, Trudy. *Pattern Bugs.*

☐ Heiligman, Deborah. *The Boy Who Loved Math: The Improbable Life of Paul Erdos.*

☐ Holub, Joan. *Zero the Hero.* Henry Holt and Co., 2012.

☐ Hulme, Joy N. *Sea Squares.*

☐ Hulme, Joy N. *Sea Sums.*

☐ Hulme, Joy N. *Wild Fibonacci.* Tricycle Press, 2010.

☐ Pinczes, Elinor J. *One Hundred Hungry Ants.* Sandpiper, 1999.

☐ Kroll, Virginia. *Equal Shmequal.* Charlesbridge Pub Inc., 2005.

☐ Leedy, Loreen. *Measuring Penny.* Square Fish, 2000.

☐ Leedy, Loreen. *Follow the Money!* Holiday House, 2003.

☐ Leedy, Loreen. *The Great Graph Contest.* Holiday House, 1999.

☐ Leedy, Loreen. *Mission: Addition.* Holiday House, 2003.

☐ Leedy, Loreen. *2 X 2 = Boo: A Set of Spooky Multiplication Stories.*

☐ Leedy, Loreen. *It's Probably Penny.* Square Fish, 2000.

☐ Leedy, Loreen. *Missing Math: A Number Mystery.* Amazon Children's Publishing, 2008.

☐ Leedy, Loreen. *Fraction Action.* Holiday House, 1996.

☐ Leedy, Loreen. *Subtraction Action.* Holiday House, 2002.

☐ Leedy, Loreen. *The Monster Money Book.* Holiday House, 2000.

☐ Lopresti, Angeline Sparagna. *A Place for Zero: A Math Adventure.*

☐ McCallum, Ann. *Rabbits Rabbits Everywhere: A Fibonacci Tale.*

☐ McGrath, Barbara Barbieri. *Teddy Bear Counting (McGrath Math).*

☐ McGrath, Barbara Barbieri. *Teddy Bear Math (McGrath Math).*

☐ McGrath, Barbara Barbieri. *Teddy Bear Patterns (McGrath Math).*

☐ McGrath, Barbara Barbieri. *Teddy Bear School Day Math (McGrath Math).*

☐ McElligott, Matthew. *The Lion's Share.* Walker Childrens, 2009.

☐ McElligott, Matthew. *Bean Thirteen.* Putnam Juvenile, 2007.

☐ Merrell, Patrick. *Pipsqueaks! Maze Party: A Book of Beginning Mazes.*

☐ Merrell, Patrick. *Pipsqueaks! Maze Day: A Book of Beginning Mazes.*

☐ Merrell, Patrick. *Pipsqueaks! Maze Halloween: A Book of Beginning Mazes.*

☐ Myller, Rolf. *How Big Is a Foot?* Yearling, 1991.

- [ ] Pinczes, Elinor J. *A Remainder of One.* Sandpiper, 2002.

- [ ] Pinczes, Elinor J. *Inchworm and A Half.* Sandpiper, 2003.

- [ ] Pinczes, Elinor J. *My Full Moon is Square.* Houghton Mifflin Books for Children, 2003.

- [ ] Pinczes, Elinor J. *One Hundred Hungry Ants.* Sandpiper, 2002.

- [ ] Schwartz, David. *If You Hopped Like a Frog.* Scholastic Press, 1999.

- [ ] Sidman, Joyce. *Swirl by Swirl: Spirals in Nature.*

- [ ] Slade, Suzanne. *What's the Difference? An Endangered Animal Subtraction Story.*

- [ ] Slade, Suzanne. *Multiply on the Fly.* Sylvan Dell Publishing, 2011.

- [ ] Souders, Taryn. *Whole-y Cow: Fractions Are Fun.* Sleeping Bear Press, 2010.

- [ ] Walton, Rick. *One More Bunny: Adding from One to Ten.* Scholastic, 2010.

- [ ] Walton, Rick. *Bunny Day: Telling Time from Breakfast to Bedtime.* Harper Collins, 2002.

- [ ] Walton, Rick. *Adventure.* Publishing, 2008.

- [ ] Wells, Robert E. *Can You Count to a Googol?*

- [ ] Wells, Robert E. *How Do You Know What Time It Is?*

- [ ] Wells, Robert E. *What's Faster Than a Speeding Cheetah?*

- [ ] Wells, Rosemary. *Bunny Money.* Puffin, 2000.

Series of Math Books (K-3rd Grades)

MathStart Level 1

- [ ] Murphy, Stuart J. *Beep Beep, Vroom Vroom! (MathStart 1).* HarperCollins, 2000.

- [ ] Murphy, Stuart J. *The Best Bug Parade (MathStart 1).* HarperCollins, 1996.

- [ ] Murphy, Stuart J. *Bug Dance (MathStart 1).* HarperCollins, 2001.

- [ ] Murphy, Stuart J. *Circus Shapes (MathStart 1).* HarperCollins, 1997.

- [ ] Murphy, Stuart J. *Double the Ducks (MathStart 1).* HarperCollins, 2002.

- [ ] Murphy, Stuart J. *Every Buddy Counts (MathStart 1).* HarperCollins, 1997.

- [ ] Murphy, Stuart J. *The Greatest Gymnast of All (MathStart 1).* HarperCollins, 1998.

- ☐ Murphy, Stuart J. *Henry the Fourth (MathStart 1)*. HarperCollins, 1998.
- ☐ Murphy, Stuart J. *A House for Birdie (MathStart 1)*. HarperCollins, 2004.
- ☐ Murphy, Stuart J. *It's About Time! (MathStart 1)*. HarperCollins, 2005.
- ☐ Murphy, Stuart J. *Jack the Builder (MathStart 1)*. HarperCollins, 2006.
- ☐ Murphy, Stuart J. *Just Enough Carrots (MathStart 1)*. HarperCollins, 1997.
- ☐ Murphy, Stuart J. *Leaping Lizards (MathStart 1)*. HarperCollins, 2005.
- ☐ Murphy, Stuart J. *Seaweed Soup (MathStart 1)*. HarperCollins, 2001.
- ☐ Murphy, Stuart J. *Mighty Maddie (MathStart 1)*. HarperCollins, 2007.
- ☐ Murphy, Stuart J. *Missing Mittens (MathStart 1)*. HarperCollins, 2000.
- ☐ Murphy, Stuart J. *Monster Musical Chairs (MathStart 1)*. HarperCollins, 2000.
- ☐ Murphy, Stuart J. *One...Two...Three... Sassafras! (MathStart 1)*. HarperCollins, 2002.
- ☐ Murphy, Stuart J. *A Pair of Socks (MathStart 1)*. HarperCollins, 1996.
- ☐ Murphy, Stuart J. *Rabbit's Pajama Party (MathStart 1)*. HarperCollins, 1999.
- ☐ Murphy, Stuart J. *3 Little Firefighters (MathStart 1)*. HarperCollins, 2003.

MathStart Level 2

- ☐ Murphy, Stuart J. *Animals on Board (MathStart 2)*. HarperCollins, 1998.
- ☐ Murphy, Stuart J. *The Best Vacation Ever (MathStart 2)*. HarperCollins, 1997.
- ☐ Murphy, Stuart J. *Bigger, Better, Best! (MathStart 2)*. HarperCollins, 2002.
- ☐ Murphy, Stuart J. *Captain Invincible and the Space Shapes (MathStart 2)*.
- ☐ Murphy, Stuart J. *Coyotes All Around (MathStart 2)*. HarperCollins, 2003.
- ☐ Murphy, Stuart J. *Elevator Magic (MathStart 2)*. HarperCollins, 1997.
- ☐ Murphy, Stuart J. *A Fair Bear Share (MathStart 2)*. HarperCollins, 1997.
- ☐ Murphy, Stuart J. *Get Up and Go! (MathStart 2)*. HarperCollins, 1996.
- ☐ Murphy, Stuart J. *Give Me Half! (MathStart 2)*. HarperCollins, 1996.
- ☐ Murphy, Stuart J. *Let's Fly a Kite (MathStart 2)*. HarperCollins, 2000.
- ☐ Murphy, Stuart J. *Mall Mania (MathStart 2)*. HarperCollins, 2006.
- ☐ Murphy, Stuart J. *More or Less (MathStart 2)*. HarperCollins, 2005.
- ☐ Murphy, Stuart J. *100 Days of Cool (MathStart 2)*. HarperCollins, 2003.

- ☐ Murphy, Stuart J. *Pepper's Journal: A Kitten's First Year (MathStart 2)*.
- ☐ Murphy, Stuart J. *Probably Pistachio (MathStart 2)*. HarperCollins, 2000.
- ☐ Murphy, Stuart J. *Racing Around (MathStart 2)*. HarperCollins, 2001.
- ☐ Murphy, Stuart J. *Same Old Horse (MathStart 2)*. HarperCollins, 2005.
- ☐ Murphy, Stuart J. *Spunky Monkeys on Parade (MathStart 2)*. HarperCollins, 1999.
- ☐ Murphy, Stuart J. *The Sundae Scoop (MathStart 2)*. HarperCollins, 2002.
- ☐ Murphy, Stuart J. *Super Sand Castle Saturday (MathStart 2)*. HarperCollins, 1998.
- ☐ Murphy, Stuart J. *Tally O'Malley (MathStart 2)*. HarperCollins, 2004.

MathStart Level 3

- ☐ Murphy, Stuart J. *Betcha! Estimating (MathStart, Level 3)*. HarperCollins, 1997.
- ☐ Murphy, Stuart J. *Dave's Down-to-Earth Rock Shop (MathStart 3)*. HarperCollins, 2000.
- ☐ Murphy, Stuart J. *Dinosaur Deals (MathStart 3)*. HarperCollins, 2001.
- ☐ Murphy, Stuart J. *Divide and Ride (MathStart 3)*. HarperCollins, 1997.
- ☐ Murphy, Stuart J. *Earth Day--Hooray! (MathStart 3)*. HarperCollins, 2004.
- ☐ Murphy, Stuart J. *Game Time! (MathStart 3)*. HarperCollins, 2000.
- ☐ Murphy, Stuart J. *Hamster Champs (MathStart 3)*. HarperCollins, 2005.
- ☐ Murphy, Stuart J. *The Grizzly Gazette (MathStart 3)*. HarperCollins, 2002.
- ☐ Murphy, Stuart J. *Jump, Kangaroo, Jump! (MathStart 3)*. HarperCollins, 1998.
- ☐ Murphy, Stuart J. *Lemonade for Sale (MathStart 3)*. HarperCollins, 1997.
- ☐ Murphy, Stuart J. *Less Than Zero (MathStart 3)*. HarperCollins, 2003.
- ☐ Murphy, Stuart J. *The Penny Pot (MathStart 3)*. HarperCollins, 1998.
- ☐ Murphy, Stuart J. *Polly's Pen Pal (MathStart 3)*. HarperCollins, 2005.
- ☐ Murphy, Stuart J. *Ready, Set, Hop! (MathStart 3)*. HarperCollins, 1996.
- ☐ Murphy, Stuart J. *Rodeo Time (MathStart 3)*. HarperCollins, 2006.
- ☐ Murphy, Stuart J. *Room for Ripley (MathStart 3)*. HarperCollins, 1999.
- ☐ Murphy, Stuart J. *Safari Park (MathStart 3)*. HarperCollins, 2001.

- ☐ Murphy, Stuart J. *Shark Swimathon (MathStart 3).* HarperCollins, 2000.
- ☐ Murphy, Stuart J. *Sluggers' Car Wash (MathStart 3).* HarperCollins, 2002.
- ☐ Murphy, Stuart J. *Treasure Map (MathStart 3).* HarperCollins, 2004.
- ☐ Murphy, Stuart J. *Too Many Kangaroo Things to Do! (MathStart 3).* HarperCollins, 1996.

A Math Adventure

- ☐ Neuschwander, Cindy. *Amanda Bean's Amazing Dream.*
- ☐ Neuschwander, Cindy. *Mummy Math: An Adventure in Geometry.*
- ☐ Neuschwander, Cindy. *Pastry School in Paris: An Adventure in Capacity.*
- ☐ Neuschwander, Cindy. *Patterns in Peru.*
- ☐ Neuschwander, Cindy. *Sir Cumference and All the King's Tens: A Math Adventure.* Charlesbridge Pub Inc., 2009.
- ☐ Neuschwander, Cindy. *Sir Cumference and the Dragon of Pi (A Math Adventure).* Charlesbridge Pub Inc., 1999.
- ☐ Neuschwander, Cindy. *Sir Cumference and the First Round Table (A Math Adventure).* Charlesbridge Pub Inc., 1997.
- ☐ Neuschwander, Cindy. *Sir Cumference and the Great Knight of Angleland (A Math Adventure).* Charlesbridge Pub Inc., 2001.
- ☐ Neuschwander, Cindy. *Sir Cumference and the Isle of Immeter (Math Adventures).* Charlesbridge Pub Inc., 2006.
- ☐ Neuschwander, Cindy. *Sir Cumference and the Off-the-Charts Dessert.*
- ☐ Neuschwander, Cindy. *Sir Cumference and the Sword in the Cone: A Math Adventure.* Charlesbridge Pub Inc., 2003.
- ☐ Neuschwander, Cindy. *Sir Cumference and the Viking's Map (Charlesbridge Math Adventures).* Charlesbridge Pub Inc., 2012.

Math is Categorical

- ☐ Cleary, Brian P. *The Mission of Addition (Math is Categorical).*
- ☐ Cleary, Brian P. *The Action of Subtraction (Math is Categorical).*

- ☐ Cleary, Brian P. *A Fraction's Goal -- Parts of a Whole (Math is Categorical)*.
- ☐ Cleary, Brian P. *How Long or How Wide?: A Measuring Guide (Math is Categorical)*.
- ☐ Cleary, Brian P. *A-B-A-B-A A Book of Pattern Play (Math is Categorical)*.
- ☐ Cleary, Brian P. *On the Scale, a Weighty Tale (Math is Categorical)*.
- ☐ Cleary, Brian P. *A Dollar, a Penny, How Much and How Many? (Math is Categorical)*.
- ☐ Cleary, Brian P. *Windows, Rings, and Grapes: A Look at Different Shapes (Math is Categorical)*.
- ☐ Cleary, Brian P. *A Second, a Minute, a Week with Days In It: A Book About Time (Math is Categorical)*.

The Warlord's Series

- ☐ Pilegard, Virginia. *The Emperor's Army: A Mathematical Adventure*.
- ☐ Pilegard, Virginia. *The Warlord's Alarm (Warlord's Series)*. Pelican Publishing, 2006.
- ☐ Pilegard, Virginia. *The Warlord's Beads (Warlord's Series)*. Pelican Publishing, 2001.
- ☐ Pilegard, Virginia. *The Warlord's Fish (Warlord's Series)*.
- ☐ Pilegard, Virginia. *The Warlord's Kites (Warlord's Series)*.
- ☐ Pilegard, Virginia. *The Warlord's Messengers (Warlord's Series)*.
- ☐ Pilegard, Virginia. *The Warlord's Puppeteers (Warlord's Series)*.
- ☐ Pilegard, Virginia. *The Warlord's Puzzle (Warlord's Series)*. Pelican Publishing, 2000.

Math Matters Series

- ☐ Aber, LInda Williams. *Carrie Measures Up (Math Matters series)*. Kane Press, 2001.
- ☐ Aber, LInda Williams. *Grandma's Button Box (Math Matters series)*. Kane Press, 2004.

☐ Aber, Linda Williams. *Who's Got Spots (Math Matters series).* Kane Press, 2000.

☐ Billin-Frye, Paige. *Clean Sweep Campers (Math Matters series).* Kane Press, 2000.

☐ Bowen, Anne. *The Great Math Tattle Battle.* Albert Whitman & Company, 2006.

☐ Bruce, Sheila. *Everybody Wins! (Math Matters series).* Kane Press, 2001.

☐ Cobb, Annie. *The Long Wait (Math Matters series).* Kane Press, 2000.

☐ DeRubertis, Donna. *A Collection for Kate (Math Matters series).* Kane Press, 1999.

☐ DeRubertis, Barbara. *Count on Pablo (Math Matters series).* Kane Press, 1999.

☐ DeRubertis, Barbara. *Deena's Lucky Penny (Math Matters Series).* Kane Press, 1999.

☐ DeRubertis, Barbara. *Lulu's Lemonade (Math Matters series).* Kane Press, 2001.

☐ Driscoll, Laura. *The Blast Off Kid (Math Matters series).* Kane Press, 2003.

☐ Dussling, Jennifer. *Fair Is Fair! (Math Matters series).* Kane Press, 2003.

☐ Dussling, Jennifer. *The 100-Pound Problem (Math Matters series).* Kane Press, 2000.

☐ Felton, Carol. *Where's Harley? (Math Matters series).* Kane Press, 2003.

☐ Friedman, Mel. *Kitten Castle (Math Matters series).* Kane Press, 2001.

☐ Gabriel, Nat. *Sam's Sneaker Squares (Math Matters series).* Kane Press, 2002.

☐ Herman, Gail. *Bad Luck Brad (Math Matters series).* Kane Press, 2002.

☐ Kassirer, Sue. *Math Fair Blues (Math Matters series).* Kane Press, 2001.

☐ Kassirer, Sue. *What's Next, Nina? (Math Matters series).* Kane Press, 2005.

☐ May, Eleanor. *Mac and Cheese, Pleeeeeze! (Math Matters series).* Kane Press, 2008.

☐ Penner, Lucille Recht. *Lights Out! (Math Matters series).* Kane Press, 2000.

☐ Penner, Lucille Recht. *Slowpoke (Math Matters series).* Kane Press, 2001.

☐ Penner, Lucille Recht. *Where's That Bone? (Math Matters series).* Kane Press, 2000.

☐ Penner, Lucille Recht. *X Marks the Spot! (Math Matters series).* Kane Press, 2002.

☐ Pitino, Donna Marie. *Too Tall Tina (Math Matters series).* Kane Press, 2005.

- [ ] Pollack, Pamela. *Chickens on the Move (Math Matters series)*. Kane Press, 2002.
- [ ] Santos, Rosa. *Play Date (Math Matters series)*. Kane Press, 2001.
- [ ] Skinner, Daphne. *All Aboard! (Math Matters series)*. Kane Press, 2007.
- [ ] Skinner, Daphne. *Tightwad Todd (Math Matters series)*. Kane Press, 2007.
- [ ] Walker, Nan. *The Yum-Yum House (Math Matters series)*. Kane Press, 2009.

Math and Logic Games (K-3rd Grades)

The Philosophy of Math Games (reference for parents)

- [ ] Kamii, Constance. *Young Children Reinvent Arithmetic: Implications of Piaget's Theory, Second Edition (Early Childhood Education Series)*.
- [ ] Kamii, Constance. *Young Children Continue to Reinvent Arithmetic: Implications of Piaget's Theory (Early Childhood Education Series)*.
- [ ] Kamii, Constance. *Young Children Continue to Reinvent Arithmetic - 3rd - Grade: Implications of Piaget's Theory (Early Childhood Education)*.

Math Games

- [ ] *Double Shutter Tin.* Blue Orange.
- [ ] *Farm Animal Counters* by Lakeshore.
- [ ] *Farkle The Classic Dice-Rolling, Risk-Taking Game.* Patch Products.
- [ ] *50 Counting Bears with 5 Cups.* Eureka School. ASIN: B0006PKZBI
- [ ] *Fraction Circles* by Lakeshore.
- [ ] *4 Way Countdown.* Ideal.
- [ ] *Geoboards* by Lakeshore.
- [ ] *Make 7.* Pressman Toy.
- [ ] *Math LInks* by Lakeshore.
- [ ] *Math War Addition and Subtraction Game Cards.* School Zone Publishing Company,
- [ ] *Math War Multiplication Game Cards.* School Zone Publishing Company.
- [ ] *Number Rings.* Orda Industries. ASIN: B000Y9TEAE

☐ *ThinkFun Math Dice Jr.* ThinkFun.

☐ *Sequence Numbers.* Jax.

☐ *7 Ate 9.* Out of the Box Publishing.

☐ *Snap It Up Math Card Game: Addition/Subtraction.* Learning Resources.

☐ *Snap It Up Math Card Game: Multiplication.* Learning Resources.

☐ *Take Ten Board Game.* Small World Toys. ASIN: B005SSQ1FM

☐ *24 Game: Add/Subtract Primer.* Suntex International. ASIN: B0009GODSK

☐ *24 Game: Multiply/Divide Primer.* Suntex International. ASIN: B0009GD084

☐ *Yahtzee.* Hasbro.

☐ *Zap!* Trend.

Logic Games

☐ *Hoppers Jr.* ThinkFun.

☐ *Izzi.* Think Fun. ASIN: B00004WJSX

☐ *Logic Links.* MindWare.

☐ *MindWare Logic Links: Level A.* MindWare.

☐ *MindWare Logic Links: Level B.* MindWare.

☐ *Noodlers.* MindWare.

☐ *Pixy Cubes.* Blue Orange. ASIN: B004P15HWG

☐ *Rush Hour Jr.* ThinkFun.

Math Music and Videos (K-3rd Grades)

Math Music

☐ *Addition Celebration* by Googol Power. ASIN: B0013PLH4O

☐ *Crazy 4 Math* by Googol Power. ASIN: B000K7LOKI

☐ *Math Tutor Addition and Subtraction* by Kidzup. ASIN: B0038FR71Y

☐ *Multiplication Vacation* by Googol Power. ASIN: B0002DUSKC

☐ *The Original Skip Count Kid Musical Multiplication Songs* by the Skip Count Kid

☐ *Skip Count Kid's Bible Heroes Musical Multiplication Songs* by the Skip Count Kid

Math Videos

☐ *School House Rock!.* Walt Disney Studios Home Entertainment.

Math Books for 4th-8th Grades

General Math Books (4th-8th Grades)

☐ Abbott, Edwin A. *Flatland.*

☐ Calvert, Pam. *Multiplying Menace: The Revenge Of Rumpelstiltskin.*

☐ Calvert, Pam. *The Multiplying Menace Divides.* Charlesbridge Pub Inc., 2011.

☐ Ekeland, Ivar. *The Cat in Numberland.*

☐ Enzensberger, Hans Magnus. *The Number Devil: A Mathematical Adventure.*

☐ Glass, Julie. A *Fly on the Ceiling (Step-Into-Reading, Step 4).*

☐ Murphy, Frank. *Ben Franklin and the Magic Squares (Step-Into-Reading, Step 4).*

☐ Packard, Edward. *Big Numbers.*

☐ Packard, Edward. *Little Numbers.*

☐ Pappas, Theoni. *The Adventures of Penrose the Mathematical Cat.*

☐ Pappas, Theoni. *Further Adventures of Penrose the Mathematical Cat.*

☐ Peterson, Ivars. *Math Trek: Adventures in the Math Zone.*

☐ Reimer, Luetta. *Mathematicians Are People Too: Stories from the Lives of Great Mathematicians, Vol. 1.*

☐ Reimer, Luetta. *Mathematicians Are People Too: Stories from the Lives of Great Mathematicians, Vol. 2.*

☐ Rosenthal, Amy Krouse Rosenthal. *Wumbers.* Chronicle Books, 2012.

☐ Schwartz, David M. *G Is for Googol: A Math Alphabet Book.*

☐ Schwartz, David M. *How Much Is a Million?* HarperCollins, 2004.

☐ Schwartz, David M. *If You Made a Million.* HarperCollins, 1994.

☐ Schwartz, David M. *Millions to Measure.* HarperCollins, 2006.

☐ Schwartz, David M. *On Beyond a Million: An Amazing Math Journey.* Dragonfly Books, 2001.

☐ Sleator, William. *The Boy Who Reversed Himself.*

- [ ] Sundby, Scott. *Cut Down to Size at High Noon: A Math Adventure.*
- [ ] Tahan, Malba. *The Man Who Counted: A Collection of Mathematical Adventures.*

Series of Math Books (4th-8th Grades)

Murderous Maths

- [ ] Poskitt, Kjartan. *Awesome Arithmetricks (Murderous Maths).*
- [ ] Poskitt, Kjartan. *Desperate Measures (Murderous Maths).*
- [ ] Poskitt, Kjartan. *Do You Feel Lucky? (Murderous Maths).*
- [ ] Poskitt, Kjartan. *Easy Questions Evil Answers (Murderous Maths).*
- [ ] Poskitt, Kjartan. *The Fiendish Angletron (Murderous Maths).*
- [ ] Poskitt, Kjartan. *Guaranteed to Bend Your Brain (Murderous Maths).*
- [ ] Poskitt, Kjartan. *Guaranteed to Mash Your Mind (Murderous Maths).*
- [ ] Poskitt, Kjartan. *Key to the Universe (Murderous Maths).*
- [ ] Poskitt, Kjartan. *The Mean and Vulgar Bits (Murderous Maths).*
- [ ] Poskitt, Kjartan. *The Perfect Sausage (Murderous Maths).*
- [ ] Poskitt, Kjartan. *Phantom X (Murderous Maths).*
- [ ] Poskitt, Kjartan. *Savage Shapes (Murderous Maths).*
- [ ] Poskitt, Kjartan. *The Secret Life of Codes (Murderous Maths).*

A Math Adventure

- [ ] Neuschwander, Cindy. *Amanda Bean's Amazing Dream.*
- [ ] Neuschwander, Cindy. *Mummy Math: An Adventure in Geometry.*
- [ ] Neuschwander, Cindy. *Pastry School in Paris: An Adventure in Capacity.*
- [ ] Neuschwander, Cindy. *Patterns in Peru.*
- [ ] Neuschwander, Cindy. *Sir Cumference and All the King's Tens: A Math Adventure.* Charlesbridge Pub Inc., 2009.
- [ ] Neuschwander, Cindy. *Sir Cumference and the Dragon of Pi (A Math Adventure).* Charlesbridge Pub Inc., 1999.
- [ ] Neuschwander, Cindy. *Sir Cumference and the First Round Table (A Math Adventure).* Charlesbridge Pub Inc., 1997.

- [ ] Neuschwander, Cindy. *Sir Cumference and the Great Knight of Angleland (A Math Adventure)*. Charlesbridge Pub Inc., 2001.
- [ ] Neuschwander, Cindy. *Sir Cumference and the Isle of Immeter (Math Adventures)*. Charlesbridge Pub Inc., 2006.
- [ ] Neuschwander, Cindy. *Sir Cumference and the Off-the-Charts Dessert*.
- [ ] Neuschwander, Cindy. *Sir Cumference and the Sword in the Cone: A Math Adventure*. Charlesbridge Pub Inc., 2003.
- [ ] Neuschwander, Cindy. *Sir Cumference and the Viking's Map (Charlesbridge Math Adventures)*. Charlesbridge Pub Inc., 2012.

Wells of Knowledge

- [ ] Wells, Robert E. *Can You Count to a Googol? (Wells of Knowledge Science)*.
- [ ] Wells, Robert E. *Did a Dinosaur Drink this Water? (Wells of Knowledge Science)*.
- [ ] Wells, Robert E. *How Do You Know What Time It Is? (Wells of Knowledge Science)*.
- [ ] Wells, Robert E. *How Do You Lift a Lion? (Wells of Knowledge Science Series)*.
- [ ] Wells, Robert E. *Is a Blue Whale the Biggest Thing There Is? (Wells of Knowledge Science)*.
- [ ] Wells, Robert E. *What's Faster Than a Speeding Cheetah? (Wells of Knowledge Science)*.
- [ ] Wells, Robert E. *What's Older Than a Giant Tortoise? (Wells of Knowledge Science)*.
- [ ] Wells, Robert E. *What's Smaller Than a Pygmy Shrew? (Wells of Knowledge Science)*.
- [ ] Wells, Robert E. *What's So Special about Planet Earth? (Wells of Knowledge Science)*.
- [ ] Wells, Robert E. *Why Do Elephants Need the Sun? (Wells of Knowledge Science)*.

Math and Logic Games (4th-8th Grades)

Math Games

- ☐ *Double Shutter Tin.* Blue Orange.
- ☐ *Farkle The Classic Dice-Rolling, Risk-Taking Game.* Patch Products.
- ☐ *Flip 4.* MindWare.
- ☐ *4 Way Countdown.* Ideal.
- ☐ *Fractiles.* Fractiles. ASIN: B00003O9KQ
- ☐ *Fraction Circles* by Lakeshore.
- ☐ *Make 7.* Pressman Toy.
- ☐ *Math War Multiplication Game Cards.* School Zone Publishing Company.
- ☐ *Sequence Numbers.* Jax.
- ☐ *7 Ate 9.* Out of the Box Publishing.
- ☐ *Snap It Up Math Card Game: Addition/Subtraction.* Learning Resources.
- ☐ *Snap It Up Math Card Game: Multiplication.* Learning Resources.
- ☐ *Sumoku.* Blue Orange.
- ☐ *Take Ten Board Game.* Small World Toys. ASIN: B005SSQ1FM
- ☐ *24 Game: Algebra/Exponents.* Suntex International. ASIN: B0006U2OFS
- ☐ *24 Game: Double Digits.* Suntex International. ASIN: B001C8G9OA
- ☐ *24 Game: Fractions/Decimals.* Suntex International. ASIN: B0009GU6IG
- ☐ *24 Game: Integers.* Suntex International. ASIN: B0006U2P70
- ☐ *24 Game: Single Digits.* Suntex International. ASIN: B002AODZFQ
- ☐ *Yahtzee.* Hasbro.
- ☐ *Zap!* Trend.
- ☐ *Zoom!* Trend.

Logic Games

- ☐ *Block by Block.* ThinkFun. ASIN: B00000IRTH
- ☐ *Brick by Brick.* ThinkFun. ASIN: B00000IRY1
- ☐ *Chocolate Fix Board Game.* ThinkFun.
- ☐ *Hoppers.* ThinkFun.

- [ ] *Izzi.* Think Fun. ASIN: B00004WJSX
- [ ] *Logic Links.* MindWare.
- [ ] *MindWare Logic Links: Level C.* MindWare.
- [ ] *MindWare Logic Links: Level D.* MindWare.
- [ ] *MindWare Word Winks.* MindWare.
- [ ] *MindWare More Word Winks.* MindWare.
- [ ] *MindWare Even More Word Winks.* MindWare.
- [ ] *Noodlers.* MindWare.
- [ ] *Pixy Cubes.* Blue Orange. ASIN: B004P15HWG
- [ ] *Rush Hour.* ThinkFun.
- [ ] *Shape by Shape.* ThinkFun. ASIN: B00000IRZ4
- [ ] *Square by Square.* ThinkFun. ASIN: B00021H92Y

Math Music and Videos (4th-8th Grades)

Math Music

- [ ] *Addition Celebration* by Googol Power. ASIN: B0013PLH4O
- [ ] *Crazy 4 Math* by Googol Power. ASIN: B000K7LOKI
- [ ] *Math Tutor Addition and Subtraction* by Kidzup. ASIN: B0038FR71Y
- [ ] *Multiplication Vacation* by Googol Power. ASIN: B0002DUSKC
- [ ] *The Original Skip Count Kid Musical Multiplication Songs* by the Skip Count Kid
- [ ] *Skip Count Kid's Bible Heroes Musical Multiplication Songs* by the Skip Count Kid

Math Videos

- [ ] *School House Rock!.* Walt Disney Studios Home Entertainment.
- [ ] *The Story of 1.* PBS Home Video.

Real Science Books

Science Books for K-3rd Grades

General Science Books (K-3rd Grades)

- ☐ Aston, Dianna Hutts. *A Butterfly is Patient.*
- ☐ Aston, Dianna Hutts. *An Egg is Quiet.*
- ☐ Aston, Dianna Hutts. *A Rock is Quiet.*
- ☐ Aston, Dianna Hutts. *A Seed is Sleepy.*
- ☐ Brendler, Carol. *Winnie Finn, Worm Farmer.*
- ☐ Berenstain, Stan and Jan. *The Berenstain Bears' Big Book of Science and Nature.* Dover Publications, 2013.
- ☐ Burgess, Thornton W. *The Burgess Animal Book for Children.*
- ☐ Burgess, Thornton W. *The Burgess Bird Book for Children.*
- ☐ Christensen, Bonnie. *I, Galileo.*
- ☐ Burleigh, Robert. *Look Up!: Henrietta Leavitt, Pioneering Woman Astronomer.*
- ☐ Fredericks, Anthony D. *Around One Cactus: Owls, Bats and Leaping Rats.*
- ☐ Fredericks, Anthony D. *Around One Log: Chipmunks, Spiders and Creepy Insiders.*
- ☐ Fredericks, Anthony D. *In One Tidepool: Crabs, Snails, and Salty Tails.*
- ☐ Fredericks, Anthony D. *On One Flower: Butterflies, Ticks and a Few More Icks.*
- ☐ Fredericks, Anthony D. *Near One Cattail: Turtles, Logs and Leaping Frogs.*
- ☐ Fredericks, Anthony D. *Under One Rock: Bugs, Slugs, and Other Ughs.*
- ☐ French, Vivian. *Yucky Worms.*
- ☐ Hawking, Lucy and Stephen. *George and the Big Bang.* Simon & Schuster Books for Young Readers, 2012.
- ☐ Hawking, Lucy and Stephen. *George's Cosmic Treasure Hunt.* Simon & Schuster Books for Young Readers, 2009.

- ☐ Hawking, Lucy and Stephen. *George's Secret Key to the Universe.* Simon & Schuster Books for Young Readers, 2007.
- ☐ Lasky, Kathryn. Pond Year.
- ☐ Leedy, Loreen. *Postcards from Pluto: A Tour of the Solar System.* Holiday House, 2006.
- ☐ Leedy, Loreen. *The Shocking Truth about Energy.* Holiday House, 2011. McNulty, Faith. *How to Dig a Hole to the Other Side of the World.* HarperCollins, 1990.
- ☐ Lunde, Darrin. *Monkey Colors.*
- ☐ Messner, Kate. *Over and Under the Snow.*
- ☐ Miller, Debbie S. *A Woolly Mammoth Journey.*
- ☐ Miller, Debbie S. *A Caribou Journey.*
- ☐ Miller, Debbie S. *A Polar Bear Journey.*
- ☐ Mortensen, Lori. *Come See the Earth Turn: The Story of Léon Foucault.*
- ☐ Nargi, Lela. *The Honeybee Man.*
- ☐ Offill, Jenny. *11 Experiments That Failed.*
- ☐ Potter, Alicia. *Mrs. Harkness and the Panda.*
- ☐ Siddals, Mary McKenna. *Compost Stew.*
- ☐ Wheeler, Lisa. *Mammoths on the Move.*
- ☐ Winter, Jeanette. *Wangari's Trees of Peace: A True Story from Africa.*

Series of Science Books (K-3rd Grades)

Cat in the Hat's Learning Library

- ☐ Rabe, Tish. *Can You See a Chimpanzee?: All About Primates (Cat in the Hat's Learning Library).*
- ☐ Rabe, Tish. *Fine Feathered Friends: All About Birds (Cat in the Hat's Learning Library).* Random House Books for Young Readers, 1998.
- ☐ Rabe, Tish. *If I Ran the Dog Show: All About Dogs (Cat in the Hat's Learning Library).* Random House Books for Young Readers, 2012.
- ☐ Rabe, Tish. *Inside Your Outside: All About the Human Body (Cat in the Hat's Learning Library).* Random House Books for Young Readers, 2003.

☐ Rabe, Tish. *Is a Camel a Mammal? (Cat in the Hat's Learning Library)*. Random House Books for Young Readers, 1998.

☐ Rabe, Tish. *Miles and Miles of Reptiles: All About Reptiles (Cat in the Hat's Learning Library)*. Random House Books for Young Readers, 2009.

☐ Rabe, Tish. *My, Oh My--A Butterfly!: All About Butterflies (Cat in the Hat's Learning Library)*. Random House Books for Young Readers, 2012.

☐ Rabe, Tish. *Oh Say Can You Say What's the Weather Today?: All About Weather (Cat in the Hat's Learning Library)*. Random House Books for Young Readers, 2004.

☐ Rabe, Tish. *Oh the Things You Can Do That Are Good for You!: All About Staying Healthy (Cat in the Hat's Learning Library)*. Random House Books for Young Readers, 2001.

☐ Rabe, Tish. *Oh, the Pets You Can Get!: All About Our Animal Friends (Cat in the Hat's Learning Library)*. Random House Books for Young Readers, 2005.

☐ Rabe, Tish. *On Beyond Bugs: All About Insects (Cat in the Hat's Learning Library)*. Random House Books for Young Readers, 1999.

☐ Rabe, Tish. *What Cat is That?: All About Cats (Cat in the Hat's Learning Library)*.

☐ Rabe, Tish. *Why Oh Why Are Deserts Dry?: All About Deserts (Cat in the Hat's Learning Library)*. Random House Books for Young Readers, 2011.

☐ Worth, Bonnie. *A Great Day for Pup! (Cat in the Hat's Learning Library)*. Random House Books for Young Readers, 2002.

☐ Worth, Bonnie. *Hark! A Shark!: All About Sharks (Cat in the Hat's Learning Library)*. Random House Books for Young Readers, 2013.

☐ Worth, Bonnie. *I Can Name 50 Trees Today!: All About Trees (Cat in the Hat's Learning Library)*. Random House Books for Young Readers, 2006.

☐ Worth, Bonnie. *Ice Is Nice!: All About the North and South Poles (Cat in the Hat's Learning Library)*. Random House Books for Young Readers, 2010.

☐ Worth, Bonnie. *If I Ran the Horse Show: All About Horses (Cat in the Hat's Learning Library)*. Random House Books for Young Readers, 2012.

☐ Worth, Bonnie. *Oh, Say Can You Say Di-no-saur? (Cat in the Hat's Learning Library)*. Random House Books for Young Readers, 1999.

- ☐ Worth, Bonnie. *Oh Say Can You Seed?: All About Flowering Plants (Cat in the Hat's Learning Library)*. Random House Books for Young Readers, 2001.
- ☐ Worth, Bonnie. *One Cent, Two Cents, Old Cent, New Cent: All About Money (Cat in the Hat's Learning Library)*. Random House Books for Young Readers, 2008.
- ☐ Worth, Bonnie. *Safari, So Good!: All About African Wildlife (Cat in the Hat's Learning Library)*. Random House Books for Young Readers, 2005.
- ☐ Worth, Bonnie. *A Whale of a Tale!: All About Porpoises, Dolphins, and Whales (Cat in the Hat's Learning Library)*. Random House Books for Young Readers, 2006.
- ☐ Worth, Bonnie. *Wish for a Fish: All About Sea Creatures (Cat in the Hat's Learning Library)*. Random House Books for Young Readers, 1999.
- ☐ Worth, Bonnie. *Would You Rather Be a Pollywog: All About Pond Life (Cat in the Hat's Learning Library)*. Random House Books for Young Readers, 2010.

Smithsonian's Backyard Books

- ☐ Brenna, Beverly. *Daddy Longlegs at Birch Lane (Smithsonian's Backyard Books)*. Soundprint, 1996.
- ☐ Dennard, Deborah. *Bullfrog at Magnolia Circle (Smithsonian's Backyard Books)*. Soundprint, 2002.
- ☐ Dennard, Deborah. *Coyote at Pinon Place (Smithsonian's Backyard Books)*. Soundprint, 1999.
- ☐ Diaz, Katacha. *Badger at Sandy Ridge Road (Smithsonian's Backyard Books)*. Soundprint, 2005.
- ☐ Galvin, Laura Gates. *Armadillo at Riverside Road (Smithsonian's Backyard Books)*. Soundprint, 1996.
- ☐ Galvin, Laura Gates. *Bumblebee at Apple Tree Lane (Smithsonian's Backyard Books)*. Soundprint, 2000.
- ☐ Galvin, Laura Gates. *Black Bear Cub at Sweet Berry Trail (Smithsonian's Backyard Books)*. Soundprint, 2008.

☐ Galvin, Laura Gates. *Deer Mouse at Old Farm Road (Smithsonian's Backyard Books)*. Soundprint, 2011.

☐ Galvin, Laura Gates. *River Otter at Autumn Lane (Smithsonian's Backyard Books)*. Soundprint, 2002.

☐ Halfmann, Janet. *Alligator at Saw Grass Road (Smithsonian's Backyard Books)*. Soundprint, 2011.

☐ Halfmann, Janet. *Canada Goose at Cattail Lane (Smithsonian's Backyard Books)*. Soundprint, 2005.

☐ Halfmann, Janet. *Garter Snake at Willow Creek Lane (Smithsonian's Backyard Books)*. Soundprint, 2011.

☐ Halfmann, Janet. *Little Black Ant on Park Street (Smithsonian's Backyard Books)*. Soundprint, 2009.

☐ Halfmann, Janet. *Red Bat at Sleepy Hollow Lane (Smithsonian's Backyard Books)*. Soundprint, 2004.

☐ Harrington, Geri. *Gray Squirrel at Pacific Avenue (Smithsonian's Backyard Books)*. Soundprint, 1995.

☐ Hollenbeck, Kathleen M. *Red Fox at Hickory Lane (Smithsonian's Backyard Books)*. Soundprint, 2011.

☐ Korman, Susan. *Groundhog at Evergreen Road (Smithsonian's Backyard Books)*. Soundprint, 2011.

☐ Korman, Susan. *Box Turtle at Silver Pond Lane (Smithsonian's Backyard Books)*. Soundprint, 2001.

☐ Lamm, C. Drew. *Cottontail at Clover Crescent (Smithsonian's Backyard Books)*. Soundprint, 1995.

☐ Lamm, C. Drew. *Screech Owl at Midnight Hollow (Smithsonian's Backyard Books)*. Soundprint, 1996.

☐ Lamm, C. Drew. *Woodchuck at Blackberry Road (Smithsonian's Backyard Books)*. Soundprint, 1994.

☐ Otto, Carolyn. *Raccoon at Clear Creek Road (Smithsonian's Backyard Books)*. Soundprint, 2011.

☐ Pfeffer, Wendy. *Firefly at Stonybrook Farm (Smithsonian's Backyard Books)*. Soundprint, 2004.

☐ Pfeffer, Wendy. *Mallard Duck at Meadow View Pond (Smithsonian's Backyard Books)*. Soundprint, 2001.

☐ Ring, Elizabeth. *Loon at Northwood Lake (Smithsonian's Backyard Books)*. Soundprint, 1997.

☐ Ring, Elizabeth. *Monarch Butterfly of Aster Way (Smithsonian's Backyard Books)*. Soundprint, 1999.

☐ Sherrow, Victoria. *Chipmunk at Hollow Tree Lane (Smithsonian's Backyard Books)*. Soundprint, 1994.

☐ Sherrow, Victoria. *Skunk at Hemlock Circle (Smithsonian's Backyard Books)*. Soundprint, 1994.

☐ Walker, Sally M. *Oppossum at Sycamore Road (Smithsonian's Backyard Books)*. Soundprint, 1997.

☐ Winkelman, Barbara. *Flying Squirrel at Acorn Place (Smithsonian's Backyard Books)*. Soundprint, 1999.

☐ Zoehfeld, Kathleen Weidner. *Fawn at Woodland Way (Smithsonian's Backyard Books)*. Soundprint, 1994.

☐ Zoehfeld, Weidner. *Ladybug at Orchard Avenue (Smithsonian's Backyard Books)*. Soundprint, 2011.

The Magic School Bus

☐ Cole, Joanna. *The Magic School Bus at the Waterworks*. Scholastic Paperbacks, 2004.

☐ Cole, Joanna. *The Magic School Bus Explores the Senses*. Scholastic Paperbacks, 2001.

☐ Cole, Joanna. *The Magic School Bus and the Electric Field Trip*. Scholastic Paperbacks, 1999.

☐ Cole, Joanna. *The Magic School Bus inside a Beehive*. Scholastic Paperbacks, 1998.

☐ Cole, Joanna. *The Magic School Bus inside a Hurricane.* Scholastic Paperbacks, 1996.

☐ Cole, Joanna. *The Magic School Bus inside the Earth.* Scholastic Paperbacks, 1989.

☐ Cole, Joanna. *The Magic School Bus inside the Human Body.* Scholastic Paperbacks, 1990.

☐ Cole, Joanna. *The Magic School Bus in the Time of the Dinosaurs.* Scholastic Paperbacks, 1995.

☐ Cole, Joanna. *The Magic School Bus Lost in the Solar System.* Scholastic Paperbacks, 1994.

☐ Cole, Joanna. *The Magic School Bus on the Ocean Floor.* Scholastic Paperbacks, 1994.

*The Following Books are from the Magic School Bus DVD Series (The books are great, but I recommend the DVD series:Magic School Bus: The Complete Series ASIN: B007I1Q4MM)

☐ Cole, Joanna. *The Magic School Bus All Dried Up: A Book about Deserts.* Scholastic Paperbacks, 1996.

☐ Cole, Joanna. *The Magic School Bus Blows its Top: A Book about Volcanoes.* Scholastic Paperbacks, 1994.

☐ Cole, Joanna. *The Magic School Bus Gets Ants in its Pants: A Book about Ants.* Scholastic Paperbacks, 1996.

☐ Cole, Joanna. *The Magic School Bus Gets Baked in a Cake: A Book about Kitchen Chemistry.* Scholastic Paperbacks, 1995.

☐ Cole, Joanna. *The Magic School Bus Gets Cold Feet: A Book about Hot-and Cold-Blooded Animals.* Scholastic Paperbacks, 1998.

☐ Cole, Joanna. *The Magic School Bus Gets Eaten: A Book about the Food Chain.* Scholastic Paperbacks, 1994.

☐ Cole, Joanna. *The Magic School Bus Gets Planted: A Book about Photosynthesis.* Scholastic Paperbacks, 1997.

☐ Cole, Joanna. *The Magic School Bus Gets Programmed: A Book about Computers.* Scholastic Paperbacks, 1999.

☐ Cole, Joanna. *The Magic School Bus Goes Upstream: A Book about Salmon Migration.* Scholastic Paperbacks, 1997.

☐ Cole, Joanna. *The Magic School Bus Going Batty: A Book about Bats.* Scholastic Paperbacks, 1996.

☐ Cole, Joanna. *The Magic School Bus in a Pickle: A Book about Microbes.* Scholastic Paperbacks, 1998.

☐ Cole, Joanna. *The Magic School Bus in the Arctic: A Book about Heat.* Scholastic Paperbacks, 1998.

☐ Cole, Joanna. *The Magic School Bus Inside Ralphie: A Book about Germs.* Scholastic Paperbacks, 1994.

☐ Cole, Joanna. *The Magic School Bus in the Haunted Museum: A Book about Sound.* Scholastic Paperbacks, 1999.

☐ White, Nancy. *The Magic School Bus Kicks Up a Storm: A Book About Weather.* Scholastic Paperbacks, 2000.

☐ Cole, Joanna. *The Magic School Bus Makes a Rainbow: A Book about Color.* Scholastic Paperbacks, 1997.

☐ Cole, Joanna. *The Magic School Bus Meets the Rot Squad: A Book About Decomposition.* Scholastic Paperbacks, 1995.

☐ Cole, Joanna. *The Magic School Bus out of this World: A Book about Space Rocks.* Scholastic Paperbacks, 1996.

☐ Cole, Joanna. *The Magic School Bus Plants a Seed.* Scholastic Paperbacks, 1995.

☐ Cole, Joanna. *The Magic School Bus Plays Ball: A Book about Forces.* Scholastic Paperbacks, 1998.

☐ Cole, Joanna. *The Magic School Bus Shows and Tells: A Book about Archaeology.* Scholastic Paperbacks, 1997.

☐ Cole, Joanna. *The Magic School Bus Spins a Web: A Book about Spiders.* Scholastic Paperbacks, 1997.

- [ ] Cole, Joanna. *The Magic School Bus Takes a Dive: A Book about Coral Reefs.* Scholastic Paperbacks, 1998.
- [ ] Cole, Joanna. *The Magic School Bus Taking Flight: A Book about Flight.* Scholastic Paperbacks, 1997.
- [ ] Cole, Joanna. *The Magic School Bus Ups and Downs: A Book about Floating and Sinking.* Scholastic Paperbacks, 1997.
- [ ] Relf, Pat. *The Magic School Bus Hops Home: A Book about Animal Habitats.* Scholastic Paperbacks, 1994.
- [ ] Relf, Pat. *The Magic School Bus Wet All Over: A Book about the Water Cycle.* Scholastic Paperbacks, 1994.
- [ ] Krulik, Nancy E. *The Magic School Bus Butterfly and the Bog Beast: A Book about Butterfly Camouflage.* Scholastic Paperbacks, 1996.
- [ ] White, Nancy. *The Magic School Bus Gets a Bright Idea: A Book about Light.* Scholastic Paperbacks, 1997.
- [ ] White, Nancy. *The Magic School Bus Sees Stars: A Book about Stars.* Scholastic Paperbacks, 1999.

Wells of Knowledge

- [ ] Wells, Robert E. *Can You Count to a Googol? (Wells of Knowledge Science).* Albert Whitman & Company, 2000.
- [ ] Wells, Robert E. *Did a Dinosaur Drink This Water? (Albert Whitman Prairie Books).* Albert Whitman & Company, 2006.
- [ ] Wells, Robert E. *How Do You Know What Time It Is? (Albert Whitman Prairie Books).* Albert Whitman & Company, 2002.
- [ ] Wells, Robert E. *How Do You Lift a Lion? (Wells of Knowledge Science).* Albert Whitman & Company, 1996.
- [ ] Wells, Robert E. *Is a Blue Whale the Biggest Thing There Is? (Wells of Knowledge Science).* Albert Whitman & Company, 1993.
- [ ] Wells, Robert E. *What's Faster Than a Speeding Cheetah? (Wells of Knowledge Science).* Albert Whitman & Company, 1997.

☐ Wells, Robert E. *What's Older Than a Giant Tortoise? (Wells of Knowledge Science).* Albert Whitman & Company, 2004.

☐ Wells, Robert E. *What's Smaller Than a Pygmy Shrew? (Wells of Knowledge Science).* Albert Whitman & Company, 1995.

☐ Wells, Robert E. *What's So Special about Planet Earth? (Wells of Knowledge Science).* Albert Whitman & Company, 2007.

☐ Wells, Robert E. *Why Do Elephants Need the Sun? (Wells of Knowledge Science).* Albert Whitman & Company, 2012.

Let's-Read-and-Find-Out-Science 1

☐ Bancroft, Henrieta. *Animals in Winter (Let's-Read-and-Find-Out Science 1).* HarperCollins, 1996.

☐ Branley, Franklyn M. *Air Is All Around You (Let's-Read-and-Find-Out Science 1).* HarperCollins, 2006.

☐ Branley, Franklyn M. *The Big Dipper (Let's-Read-and-Find-Out Science 1).* HarperCollins, 1991.

☐ Bulla, Clyde Robert. *A Tree Is a Plant (Let's-Read-and-Find-Out Science 1).* HarperCollins, 2001.

☐ Esbensen, Barbara Juster. *Baby Whales Drink Milk (Let's-Read-and-Find-Out Science 1).* HarperCollins, 1994.

☐ Fraser, Mary Ann. *Where Are the Night Animals? (Let's-Read-and-Find-Out Science 1).* HarperCollins, 1998.

☐ Hurd, Edith Thacher. *Starfish (Let's-Read-and-Find-Out Science 1).* HarperCollins, 2000.

☐ Jenkins, Priscilla Beiz. *A Nest Full of Eggs (Let's-Read-and-Find-Out Science 1).* HarperCollins, 1995.

☐ Jordan, Helene J. *How a Seed Grows (Let's-Read-and-Find-Out Science 1).* HarperCollins, 1992.

☐ Pfeffer, Wendy. *From Tadpole to Frog (Let's-Read-and-Find-Out Science 1).* HarperCollins, 1994.

☐ Pfeffer, Wendy. *Sounds All Around (Let's-Read-and-Find-Out Science 1)*. HarperCollins, 1998.

☐ Pfeffer, Wendy. *What's It Like to Be a Fish? (Let's-Read-and-Find-Out Science 1)*. HarperCollins, 1996.

☐ Rockwell, Anne. *Bugs Are Insects (Let's-Read-and-Find-Out Science 1)*. HarperCollins, 2001.

☐ Rockwell, Anne. *Clouds (Let's-Read-and-Find-Out Science 1)*. HarperCollins, 2008.

☐ Selsam, Millicent E. *Big Tracks, Little Tracks: Following Animal Prints (Let's-Read-and-Find-Out Science, Stage 1)*. HarperCollins, 1998.

☐ Showers, Paul. *How Many Teeth? (Let's-Read-and-Find-Out Science 1)*. HarperCollins, 2004.

☐ Sklansky, Amy E. *Where Do Chicks Come From? (Let's-Read-and-Find-Out Science 1)*. HarperCollins, 2005.

☐ Zoehfeld, Kathleen Weidner. *Dinosaurs Big and Small (Let's-Read-and-Find-Out Science, Stage 1)*. HarperCollins, 2002.

☐ Zoehfeld, Kathleen Weidner. *What Lives in a Shell? (Let's-Read-and-Find-Out Science 1)*. HarperCollins, 1994.

☐ Zoehfeld, Kathleen Weidner. *What's Alive? (Let's-Read-and-Find-Out Science 1)*. HarperCollins, 1995.

Let's-Read-and-Find-Out-Science 2

☐ Aliki. *Digging Up Dinosaurs (Let's-Read-and-Find-Out Science 2)*. HarperCollins, 1988.

☐ Aliki. *Dinosaurs Are Different (Let's-Read-and-Find-Out Science 2)*. HarperCollins, 1986.

☐ Aliki. *Dinosaur Bones (Let's-Read-and-Find-Out Science 2)*. HarperCollins, 1990.

☐ Aliki. *Fossils Tell of Long Ago (Let's-Read-and-Find-Out Science 2)*. HarperCollins, 1990.

☐ Aliki. *My Visit to the Dinosaurs (Let's-Read-and-Find-Out Science 2).* HarperCollins, 1985.

☐ Balestrino, Philip. *The Skeleton Inside You (Let's-Read-and-Find-Out Science 2).* HarperCollins, 1989.

☐ Berger, Melvin. *Chirping Crickets (Let's-Read-and-Find-Out Science, Stage 2).* HarperCollins, 2004.

☐ Berger, Melvin. *Germs Make Me Sick! (Let's-Read-and-Find-Out Science 2).* HarperCollins, 1995.

☐ Berger, Melvin. *Spinning Spiders (Let's-Read-and-Find-Out Science 2).* HarperCollins, 2003.

☐ Berger, Melvin. *Switch On, Switch Off (Let's-Read-and-Find-Out Science 2).* HarperCollins, 1990.

☐ Berger, Melvin. *Why I Sneeze, Shiver, Hiccup, & Yawn (Let's-Read-and-Find-Out Science 2).* HarperCollins, 2000.

☐ Bradley, Kimberly Brubaker. *Energy Makes Things Happen (Let's-Read-and-Find-Out Science 2).* HarperCollins, 2002.

☐ Bradley, Kimberly Brubaker. *Forces Make Things Move (Let's-Read-and-Find-Out Science 2).* HarperCollins, 2005.

☐ Branley, Frank M. *Day Light, Night Light: Where Light Comes From (Let's-Read-and-Find-Out Science 2).* HarperCollins, 1998.

☐ Branley, Franklyn M. *Down Comes the Rain (Let's-Read-and-Find-Out Science 2).* HarperCollins, 2004.

☐ Branley, Franklyn M. *Earthquakes (Let's-Read-and-Find-Out Science 2).* HarperCollins, 2005.

☐ Branley, Franklyn M. *Flash, Crash, Rumble, and Roll (Let's-Read-and-Find-Out Science 2).* HarperCollins, 1999.

☐ Branley, Franklyn M. *Floating in Space (Let's-Read-and-Find-Out Science 2).* HarperCollins, 1998.

☐ Branley, Franklyn M. *Gravity Is a Mystery (Let's-Read-And-Find-Out Science 2).* HarperCollins, 2007.

☐ Branley, Frank M. *The International Space Station (Let's-Read-and-Find-Out Science 2).* HarperCollins, 2000.

☐ Branley, Frank M. *Mission to Mars (Let's-Read-and-Find-Out Science 2).* HarperCollins, 2002.

☐ Branley, Franklyn M. *The Moon Seems to Change (Let's-Read-and-Find-Out Science 2).* HarperCollins, 1987.

☐ Branley, Franklyn M. *The Planets in Our Solar System (Let's-Read-and-Find-Out Science, Stage 2).* HarperCollins, 2004.

☐ Branley, Frank M. *The Sky Is Full of Stars (Let's-Read-and-Find-Out Science 2).* HarperCollins, 1983

☐ Branley, Franklyn M. *The Sun: Our Nearest Star (Let's-Read-and-Find-Out).* HarperCollins, 2002.

☐ Branley, Franklyn M. *Sunshine Makes the Seasons (Let's-Read-and-Find-Out Science 2).* HarperCollins, 2005.

☐ Branley, Franklyn M. *Tornado Alert (Let's-Read-and-Find-Out Science 2).* HarperCollins, 1990.

☐ Branley, Franklyn M. *Volcanoes (Let's-Read-and-Find-Out Science 2).* HarperCollins, 2008.

☐ Branley, Frank M. *What the Moon is Like (Let's-Read-and-Find-Out Science, Stage 2).* HarperCollins, 2000.

☐ Branley, Franklyn M. *What Happened to the Dinosaurs? (Let's-Read-and-Find-Out Science 2).* HarperCollins, 1991.

☐ Branley, Franklyn M. *What Makes Day and Night (Let's-Read-and-Find-Out Science 2).* HarperCollins, 1986.

☐ Branley, Franklyn M. *What Makes a Magnet? (Let's-Read-and-Find-Out Science 2).* HarperCollins, 1996.

☐ DeWitt, Lynda. *What Will the Weather Be? (Let's-Read-and-Find-Out Science 2).* HarperCollins, 2004.

☐ Dorros, Arthur. *Ant Cities (Let's-Read-and-Find-Out Science 2).* HarperCollins, 1988.

☐ Dorros, Arthur. *Feel the Wind (Let's-Read-and-Find-Out Science 2)*. HarperCollins, 1990.

☐ Dorros, Arthur. *Follow the Water from Brook to Ocean (Let's-Read-and-Find-Out Science 2)*. HarperCollins, 1993.

☐ Duke, Kate. *Archaeologists Dig for Clues (Let's-Read-and-Find-Out Science 2)*. HarperCollins, 1996.

☐ Earle, Ann. *Zipping, Zapping, Zooming Bats (Let's-Read-and-Find-Out Science 2)*. HarperCollins, 1995.

☐ Gans, Roma. *How Do Birds Find Their Way? (Let's-Read-and-Find-Out Science 2)*. HarperCollins, 1996.

☐ Gans, Roma. *Let's Go Rock Collecting (Let'S-Read-And-Find-Out Science 2)*. HarperCollins, 1997.

☐ Hodgkins, Fran. *How People Learned to Fly (Let's-Read-and-Find-Out Science 2)*. HarperCollins, 2007.

☐ Lauber, Patricia. *An Octopus Is Amazing (Let's-Read-and-Find-Out Science 2)*. HarperCollins, 1996.

☐ Lauber, Patricia. *Snakes Are Hunters (Let's-Read-and-Find-Out Science 2)*. HarperCollins, 1989.

☐ Lauber, Patricia. Who Eats What? Food Chains and Food Webs (Let's-Read-and-Find-Out Science 2). HarperCollins, 1994.

☐ Maestro, Betsy. *How Do Apples Grow? (Let's-Read-and-Find-Out Science 2)*. HarperCollins, 1993.

☐ Maestro, Betsy. *Why Do Leaves Change Color? (Let's-Read-and-Find-Out Science 2)*. HarperCollins, 1994.

☐ Otto, Carolyn B. *What Color Is Camouflage? (Let's-Read-and-Find-Out Science 2)*. HarperCollins, 1996.

☐ Pfeffer, Wendy. *Dolphin Talk: Whistles, Clicks, and Clapping Jaws (Let's-Read-and-Find-Out Science, Stage 2)*. HarperCollins, 2003.

☐ Pfeffer, Wendy. *Life in a Coral Reef (Let's-Read-and-Find-Out Science 2)*. HarperCollins, 2004.

☐ Pfeffer, Wendy. *Wiggling Worms at Work (Let's-Read-and-Find-Out Science 2)*. HarperCollins, 2003.

☐ Showers, Paul. *A Drop of Blood (Let's-Read-and-Find-Out Science 2)*. HarperCollins, 2004.

☐ Showers, Paul. *Hear Your Heart (Let's-Read-and-Find-Out Science 2)*. HarperCollins, 2000.

☐ Showers, Paul. *What Happens to a Hamburger? (Let's-Read-and-Find-Out Science 2)*. HarperCollins, 2001.

☐ Showers, Paul. *Where Does the Garbage Go? (Let's-Read-and-Find-Out Science 2)*. HarperCollins, 1994.

☐ Showers, Paul. *Your Skin and Mine: Revised Edition (Let's-Read-and-Find-Out Science 2)*. HarperCollins, 1991.

☐ Tatham, Betty. *Penguin Chick (Let's-Read-and-Find-Out Science 2)*. HarperCollins, 2001.

☐ Zoehfeld, Kathleen Weldner. *Did Dinosaurs Have Feathers? (Let's-Read-and-Find-Out Science 2)*. HarperCollins, 2003.

☐ Zoehfeld, Kathleen Weldner. *Dinosaur Tracks (Let's-Read-and-Find-Out Science 2)*. HarperCollins, 2007.

☐ Zoehfeld, Kathleen Weldner. *How Mountains Are Made (Let's-Read-and-Find-Out Science 2)*. HarperCollins, 1995.

☐ Zoehfeld, Kathleen Weidner. *What Is the World Made Of? All About Solids, Liquids, and Gases (Let's-Read-and-Find-Out Science 2)*. HarperCollins, 1998.

☐ Zoehfeld, Kathleen Weldner. *Where Did Dinosaurs Come From? (Let's-Read-and-Find-Out Science 2)*. HarperCollins, 2010.

Science Videos K-3rd Grade

Magic School Bus (There are around 50 episodes of the Magic School bus; by far the most economical way to purchase them are in the complete series below.)

☐ *Magic School Bus: The Complete Series (DVD)*. ASIN: B007I1Q4MM

☐ *The Magic School Bus: Gets Lost in Space (space)*

- [ ] *The Magic School Bus: For Lunch (digestion)*
- [ ] *The Magic School Bus: Inside Ralphie (germs)*
- [ ] *The Magic School Bus: Gets Eaten (food chain)*
- [ ] *The Magic School Bus: Hops Home (animal habitats)*
- [ ] *The Magic School Bus: Meets the Rot Squad (decomposition)*
- [ ] *The Magic School Bus: All Dried Up (deserts)*
- [ ] *The Magic School Bus: In the Haunted Hosue (sound)*
- [ ] *The Magic School Bus: Gets Ready, Set, Dough (kitchen chemistry)*
- [ ] *The Magic School Bus: Plays Ball (forces)*
- [ ] *The Magic School Bus: Goes to Seed (seeds)*
- [ ] *The Magic School Bus: Kicks up a Storm (weather)*
- [ ] *The Magic School Bus: Blows Its Top (volcanoes)*
- [ ] *The Magic School Bus: Flexes Its Muscles (body mechanics)*
- [ ] *The Magic School Bus: The Busasaurus (dinosaurs)*
- [ ] *The Magic School Bus: Going Batty (bats)*
- [ ] *The Magic School Bus: Butterfly and the Bog Beast (butterflies)*
- [ ] *The Magic School Bus: Wet All Over (water cycle)*
- [ ] *The Magic School Bus: In a Pickle (microbes)*
- [ ] *The Magic School Bus: Revving Up (engines)*
- [ ] *The Magic School Bus: Taking Flight (flight)*
- [ ] *The Magic School Bus: Getting Energized (energy)*
- [ ] *The Magic School Bus: Out of this World (space)*
- [ ] *The Magic School Bus: Cold Feet (warm and cold blooded animals)*
- [ ] *The Magic School Bus: Ups and Downs (floating and sinking)*
- [ ] *The Magic School Bus: In a Beehive (bees)*
- [ ] *The Magic School Bus: In the Arctic (heat)*
- [ ] *The Magic School Bus: Spins a Web (spiders)*
- [ ] *The Magic School Bus: Under Construction (structures)*
- [ ] *The Magic School Bus: Gets a Bright Idea (light)*
- [ ] *The Magic School Bus: Shows and Tells (archaeology)*
- [ ] *The Magic School Bus: Makes a Rainbow (color)*

- [ ] *The Magic School Bus: Goes Upstream (salmon migration)*
- [ ] *The Magic School Bus: Works Out (circulation)*
- [ ] *The Magic School Bus: Gets Planted (photosynthesis)*
- [ ] *The Magic School Bus: In the Rainforest (rainforest ecology)*
- [ ] *The Magic School Bus: Rocks and Rolls (water erosion)*
- [ ] *The Magic School Bus: Holiday Special (recycling)*
- [ ] *The Magic School Bus: Meets Molly Cule (molecules)*
- [ ] *The Magic School Bus: Cracks a Yolk (eggs)*
- [ ] *The Magic School Bus: Goes to Mussel Beach (tidal zones)*
- [ ] *The Magic School Bus: Goes on Air (air pressure)*
- [ ] *The Magic School Bus: Gets Swamped (wetlands)*
- [ ] *The Magic School Bus: Goes Cellular (cells)*
- [ ] *The Magic School Bus: Sees Stars (stars)*
- [ ] *The Magic School Bus: Gains Weight (gravity)*
- [ ] *The Magic School Bus: Makes a Stink (smell)*
- [ ] *The Magic School Bus: Gets Charged (electricity)*
- [ ] *The Magic School Bus: Gets Programmed (computers)*
- [ ] *The Magic School Bus: In the City (city critters)*
- [ ] *The Magic School Bus: Takes a Dive (coral reefs)*

See How They Grow (This is a wonderful series in the style of the DK Eyewitness videos that watches the development of different species from infant to adult. At the moment these are only available on VHS; I'm hoping that they will update this series to DVD sometime soon.)

- [ ] *See How They Grow: Desert Animals*
- [ ] *See How They Grow: Forest Animals*
- [ ] *See How They Grow: Insects and Spiders*
- [ ] *See How They Grow: Jungle Animals*
- [ ] *See How They Grow: Pets*
- [ ] *See How They Grow: Pond Animals*

- [ ] *See How They Grow: Sea Animals*
- [ ] *See How They Grow: Tree Animals*
- [ ] *See How They Grow: Wild Animals*

Zoboomafoo (Martin and Chris Kratt) (One of the best children's educational shows produced by PBS. My son adored this show. Unfortunately not all of the 65 episodes were released for sale on VHS and fewer are available on DVD. I'm hoping enough people will ask PBS to replay or release this series that it will become available in its entirety.)

- [ ] *Zoboomafoo: With the Kratt Brothers DVD.* ASIN: B001T8EL1Q (6 episodes)
  - [ ] *Zoboomafoo: Fling*
  - [ ] *Zoboomafoo: Slimy Buddies*
  - [ ] *Zoboomafoo: Fast and Slow*
  - [ ] *Zoboomafoo: Giants*
  - [ ] *Zoboomafoo: Bears*
  - [ ] *Zoboomafoo: Eye Spy*

Wild Kratts (Martin and Chris Kratt) (Available on Amazon Prime Instant Video and Netflix. Arranged in order of production.)

- [ ] *Wild Kratts: Mom of a Croc.*
- [ ] *Wild Kratts: Whale of a Squid.*
- [ ] *Wild Kratts: Aardvark Town*
- [ ] *Wild Kratts: Flight of the Draco.*
- [ ] *Wild Kratts: Mystery of the Squirmy Wormy.*
- [ ] *Wild Kratts: Platypus Café.*
- [ ] *Wild Kratts: Build it Beaver.*
- [ ] *Wild Kratts: Voyage of the Butterflier XT.*
- [ ] *Wild Kratts: Honey Seekers.*
- [ ] *Wild Kratts: Bass Class.*
- [ ] *Wild Kratts: Fireflies.*

- [ ] *Wild Kratts: Mystery of the Weird Looking Walrus.*
- [ ] *Wild Kratts: Tazzy Chris.*
- [ ] *Wild Kratts: Octopus Wildkratticus.*
- [ ] *Wild Kratts: Walk on the Wet Side.*
- [ ] *Wild Kratts: Elephant in the Room.*
- [ ] *Wild Kratts: Let the Rhinos Roll!*
- [ ] *Wild Kratts: Kickin' it with the Roos.*
- [ ] *Wild Kratts: The Blue and the Gray.*
- [ ] *Wild Kratts: Falcon City.*
- [ ] *Wild Kratts: Polar Bears don't Dance.*
- [ ] *Wild Kratts: Koala Balloon.*
- [ ] *Wild Kratts: Cheetah Racer.*
- [ ] *Wild Kratts: Kerhonk.*
- [ ] *Wild Kratts: Mimic.*
- [ ] *Wild Kratts: Caracal-minton.*
- [ ] *Wild Kratts: Zig-zagged.*
- [ ] *Wild Kratts: A Huge Orange Problem.*
- [ ] *Wild Kratts: The Food Chain Game.*
- [ ] *Wild Kratts: Masked Bandits.*
- [ ] *Wild Kratts: Seasquatch.*
- [ ] *Wild Kratts: Flight of the Polinators.*
- [ ] *Wild Kratts: The Gecko Effect.*
- [ ] *Wild Kratts: LIttle Howler.*
- [ ] *Wild Kratts: Quillber's Birthday Present.*
- [ ] *Wild Kratts: A Bat in the Brownies.*
- [ ] *Wild Kratts: Stuck on Sharks.*
- [ ] *Wild Kratts: Birds of a Feather.*
- [ ] *Wild Kratts: Googly Eye: The Night Guru.*
- [ ] *Wild Kratts: Raptor Round Up*

Science Books for 4th-8th Grades

General Science Books (4th-8th Grade)

- ☐ Bardoe, Cheryl. *The Gregor Mendel: Friar Who Grew Peas.* Harry N. Abrams, 2006.

- ☐ Barton, Chris. *The Day-Glo Brothers.* Charlesbridge Publishing, 2009.

- ☐ Brown, Don. *Odd Boy Out: Young Albert Einstein.* Houghton Mifflin Books for Children, 2004.

- ☐ Brown, Don. *A Wizard from the Start: The Incredible Boyhood and Amazing Inventions of Thomas Edison.* Houghton Mifflin Books for Children, 2010.

- ☐ Christensen, Bonnie. *I, Galileo.*

- ☐ Davies, Jacqueline. *The Boy Who Drew Birds: A Story of John James Audubon.* Houghton Mifflin Books for Children, 2004.

- ☐ Davies, Nicola. *Extreme Animals: The Toughest Animals on Earth.*

- ☐ Davies, Nicola. *Just the Right Size: Why Big Animal are Big and Little Animals are Little.*

- ☐ Davies, Nicola. *Poop: A Natural History of the Unmentionable.*

- ☐ Davies, Nicola. *What's Eating You?: Parasites -- The Inside Story.*

- ☐ Floca, Brian. *The Moonshot: Flight of Apollo 11.* Atheneum/Richard Jackson Books, 2009.

- ☐ Fradin, Dennis B. *Nicolaus copernicus: The Earth is a Planet.* Mondo Pub, 2004.

- ☐ Goodman, Susan. *Gee Whiz! It's All About Pee.*

- ☐ Goodman, Susan. *The Truth About Poop.*

- ☐ Hatkoff, Isabella. *Owen & Mzee: The True Story of a Remarkable Friendship.*

- ☐ Holland, Jennifer. *Unlikely Friendships: 47 Remarkable Stories from the Animal Kingdom.* ISBN-13: 978-0761159131

- ☐ Hoose, Phillip. *Moonbird: A Year on the Wind with the Great Survivor B95.*

- ☐ Jones, Charlotte. *Mistakes That Worked.* Doubleday Books for Young Readers, 1994.

- ☐ Krull, Kathleen. *The Boy Who Invented TV: The Story of Philo Farnsworth.* Knopf Books for Young Readers, 2009.

☐ Lasky, Kathryn. *The Librarian Who Measured the Earth.* Little, Brown Books for Young Readers, 2001.

☐ Lasky, Kathryn. *The Man Who Made Time Travel.* Farrar, Straus and Giroux, 2003.

☐ Lasky, Kathryn. *The Most Beautiful Roof in the World.*

☐ Lasky, Kathryn. *One Beetle Too Many: The Extraordinary Adventures of Charles Darwin.* Candlewick Press, 2013.

☐ MacDonald, Wendy. *Galileo's Leaning Tower Experiment.* Charlesbridge Publishing, 2009.

☐ Martin, Jacqueline Briggs. *Snowflake Bentley.* Houghton Mifflin Books for Children, 2009.

☐ McCarthy, Meghan. *Pop!: The Invention of Bubble Gum.* Publishing, 2008.

☐ McCully, Emily Arnold. *Marvelous Mattie: How Margaret E. Knight Became an Inventor.* Farrar, Straus & Giroux, 2006.

☐ Mortensen, Lori. *Come See the Earth Turn: The Story of Léon Foucault.*

☐ Nivola, Claire A. *Life in the Ocean: The Story of Oceanographer Sylvia Earle.*

☐ Nivola, Claire A. *Planting the Trees of Kenya: The Story of Wangari Maathai.* Platt, Richard. *Plagues, Pox, and Pestilence.* ISBN 0753466872

☐ Sis, Peter. *Starry Messenger: Galileo Galilei.* HarperCollins, 2004.

☐ Stannard, Russell. *Black Holes and Uncle Albert.* Faber Childrens, 2005.

☐ Stannard, Russell. *Time and Space of Uncle Albert.* Faber Childrens, 2005.

☐ Stannard, Russell. *Uncle Albert and the Quantum Quest.* Faber Childrens, 2005.

☐ Stone, Tanya Lee. *Who Says Women Can't Be Doctors?: The Story of Elizabeth Blackwell.*

☐ Winter, Jeanette. *The Watcher: Jane Goodall's Life with the Chimps.* Schwartz & Wade, 2011.

☐ Wulffson, Don L. *The Kid Who Invented the Popsicle: And Other Surprising Stories about Inventions.* Puffin, 1999.

☐ Wulffson, Don L. *Toys!: Amazing Stories Behind Some Great Inventions.* Henry Holt and Co., 2000.

Series of Science Books (4th-8th Grades)

Getting to Know the World's Greatest Inventors and Scientists

- ☐ Venezia, Mike. *Albert Einstein: Universal Genius (Getting to Know the World's Greatest Inventors & Scientists).* Children's Press, 2009.

- ☐ Venezia, Mike. *Alexander Graham Bell: Setting the Tone for Communication (Getting to Know the World's Greatest Inventors & Scientists).* Children's Press, 2009.

- ☐ Venezia, Mike. *Benjamin Franklin: Electrified the World with New Ideas (Getting to Know the World's Greatest Inventors & Scientists).* Children's Press, 2010.

- ☐ Venezia, Mike. *Charles Drew: Doctor Who Got the World Pumped Up to Donate Blood (Getting to Know the World's Greatest Inventors and Scientists).* Children's Press, 2009.

- ☐ Venezia, Mike. *Daniel Hale Williams: Surgeon Who Opened Hearts and Minds (Getting to Know the World's Greatest Inventors & Scientists).* Children's Press, 2010.

- ☐ Venezia, Mike. *Henry Ford: Big Wheel in the Auto Industry (Getting to Know the World's Greatest Inventors & Scientists).* Children's Press, 2009.

- ☐ Venezia, Mike. *Jane Goodall: Researcher Who Champions Chimps (Getting to Know the World's Greatest Inventors & Scientists).* Children's Press, 2010.

- ☐ Venezia, Mike. *Lise Meitner: Had the Right Vision About Nuclear Fission (Getting to Know the World's Greatest Inventors and Scientists).* Children's Press, 2010.

- ☐ Venezia, Mike. *Luis Alvarez: Wild Idea Man (Getting to Know the World's Greatest Inventors & Scientists).* Children's Press, 2010.

- ☐ Venezia, Mike. *Marie Curie: Scientist Who Made Glowing Discoveries (Getting to Know the World's Greatest Inventors & Scientists).* Children's Press, 2009.

- ☐ Venezia, Mike. *Mary Leakey: Archaeologist Who Really Dug Her Work (Getting to Know the World's Greatest Inventors & Scientists).* Children's Press, 2009.

- ☐ Venezia, Mike. *Rachel Carson: Clearing the Way for Environmental Protection (Getting to Know the World's Greatest Inventors & Scientists).* Children's Press, 2010.

- [ ] Venezia, Mike. *Stephen Hawking: Cosmologist Who Gets a Big Bang Out of the Universe (Getting to Know the World's Greatest Inventors & Scientists).* Children's Press, 2009.
- [ ] Venezia, Mike. *Steve Jobs & Steve Wozniak: Geek Heroes Who Put the Personal in Computers (Getting to Know the World's Greatest Inventors and Scientists).* Children's Press, 2010.
- [ ] Venezia, Mike. *Thomas Edison: Inventor With a Lot of Bright Ideas (Getting to Know the World's Greatest Inventors and Scientists).* Children's Press, 2009.
- [ ] Venezia, Mike. *The Wright Brothers: Inventors Whose Ideas Really Took Flight (Getting to Know the World's Greatest Inventors and Scientists).* Children's Press, 2010.

Enjoy Your Cells/Cells and Things

- [ ] Balkwill, Fran. *Enjoy Your Cells (Enjoy Your Cells, 1).* Cold Spring Harbor Laboratory Press, 2001.
- [ ] Balkwill, Fran. *Germ Zappers (Enjoy Your Cells, 2).* Cold Spring Harbor Laboratory Press, 2001.
- [ ] Balkwill, Fran. *Have a Nice DNA (Enjoy Your Cells, 3).* Cold Spring Harbor Laboratory Press, 2002.
- [ ] Balkwill, Fran. *Gene Machines (Enjoy Your Cells, 4).* Cold Spring Harbor Laboratory Press, 2002.
- [ ] Balkwill, Fran. *Amazing Schemes Within Your Genes (Cells and Things).* Carolrhoda Books, 1993.
- [ ] Balkwill, Fran. *Cell Wars (Cells and Things).* First Avenue Editions, 1990.
- [ ] Balkwill, Fran. *DNA is Here to Stay (Cells and Things).* Carolrhoda Books, 1994.

Horrible Science

- [ ] Arnold, Nick. *Angry Animals (Horrible Science).* Scholastic, 2008.
- [ ] Arnold, Nick. *Blood, Bones and Body Bits (Horrible Science).* Scholastic, 2008.

☐ Arnold, Nick. *Body Owner's Handbook (Horrible Science)*. Scholastic, 2008.

☐ Arnold, Nick. *Bulging Brains (Horrible Science)*. Scholastic, 2008.

☐ Arnold, Nick. *Chemical Chaos (Horrible Science)*. Scholastic, 2008.

☐ Arnold, Nick. *Deadly Diseases (Horrible Science)*. Scholastic, 2008.

☐ Arnold, Nick. *Disgusting Digestion (Horrible Science)*. Scholastic, 2008.

☐ Arnold, Nick. *Evil Inventions (Horrible Science)*. Scholastic, 2004.

☐ Arnold, Nick. *Evolve or Die (Horrible Science)*. Scholastic, 2008.

☐ Arnold, Nick. *Explosive Experiments (Horrible Science)*. Scholastic, 2008.

☐ Arnold, Nick. *Fatal Forces (Horrible Science)*. Scholastic, 2008.

☐ Arnold, Nick. *The Fight for Flight (Horrible Science)*. Scholastic, 2008.

☐ Arnold, Nick. *Frightening Light (Horrible Science)*. Scholastic, 2008.

☐ Arnold, Nick. *Killer Energy (Horrible Science)*. Scholastic, 2008.

☐ Arnold, Nick. *Nasty Nature (Horrible Science)*. Scholastic, 2008.

☐ Arnold, Nick. *Microscopic Monsters (Horrible Science)*. Scholastic, 2008.

☐ Arnold, Nick. *Painful Poison (Horrible Science)*. Scholastic, 2008.

☐ Arnold, Nick. *Really Rotten Experiments (Horrible Science)*. Scholastic, 2008.

☐ Arnold, Nick. *Shocking Electricity (Horrible Science)*. Scholastic, 2008.

☐ Arnold, Nick. *Sick! From Measly Medicine to Savage Surgery (Horrible Science)*. Scholastic, 2008.

☐ Arnold, Nick. *Sounds Dreadful (Horrible Science)*. Scholastic, 2008.

☐ Arnold, Nick. *Space, Stars and Slimy Aliens (Horrible Science)*. Scholastic, 2008.

☐ Arnold, Nick. *Suffering Scientists (Horrible Science)*. Scholastic, 2008.

☐ Arnold, Nick. *Terrible Truth about Time (Horrible Science)*. Scholastic, 2008.

☐ Arnold, Nick. *Ugly Bugs (Horrible Science)*. Scholastic, 2008.

☐ Arnold, Nick. *Vicious Veg (Horrible Science)*. Scholastic, 2008.

☐ Arnold, Nick. *Wasted World (Horrible Science)*. Scholastic, 2008.

Dr. Joe Schwarcz

☐ Schwarcz, Joe Dr. *The Fly in the Ointment: 70 Fascinating Commentaries on the Science of Everyday Life*. ECW Press, 2004.

- Schwarcz, Joe Dr. *The Genie in the Bottle: 67 All-New Commentaries on the Fascinating Chemistry of Everyday Life.* Holt Paperbacks, 2002.
- Schwarcz, Joe Dr. *Let Them Eat Flax: 70 All-New Commentaries on the Science of Everyday Food & Life.* ECW Press, 2005.
- Schwarcz, Joe Dr. *Radar, Hula Hoops, and Playful Pigs: 67 Digestible Commentaries on the Fascinating Chemistry of Everyday Life.* Holt Paperbacks, 2001.
- Schwarcz, Joe Dr. *That's the Way the Cookie Crumbles: 62 All-New Commentaries on the Fascinating Chemistry of Everyday Life.* ECW Press, 2002.

Science Music (4th-8th Grades)

Lyrical Learning (Hard copy CDs and digital downloads can be found at lyricallearning.com)
- Eldon, Doug. *Lyrical Life Science: Bacteria to Birds - Volume 1.*
- Eldon, Doug. *Lyrical Life Science: Mammals, Ecology and Biomes - Volume 2.*
- Eldon, Doug. *Lyrical Life Science: The Human Body - Volume 3.*
- Eldon, Doug. *Lyrical Earth Science: Geology.*

Science Videos (4th-8th Grades)

Bill Nye the Science Guy (Hands down the best science series for students in late elementary and middle grades. They are a bit pricey, but worth every penny. A few of these DVDs can be found on amazon.com and ebay.com, but for most of them, the best place is billnye.com)
- *Bill Nye the Science Guy: Amphibians.*
- *Bill Nye the Science Guy: Animal Locomotion.*
- *Bill Nye the Science Guy: Archaeology.*
- *Bill Nye the Science Guy: Architecture.*
- *Bill Nye the Science Guy: Atmosphere.*
- *Bill Nye the Science Guy: Atoms.*

- ☐ *Bill Nye the Science Guy: Balance.*
- ☐ *Bill Nye the Science Guy: Biodiversity.*
- ☐ *Bill Nye the Science Guy: Birds.*
- ☐ *Bill Nye the Science Guy: Blood and Circulation.*
- ☐ *Bill Nye the Science Guy: Bones and Muscles.*
- ☐ *Bill Nye the Science Guy: Brain.*
- ☐ *Bill Nye the Science Guy: Buoyancy.*
- ☐ *Bill Nye the Science Guy: Caves.*
- ☐ *Bill Nye the Science Guy: Cells.*
- ☐ *Bill Nye the Science Guy: Chemical Reactions.*
- ☐ *Bill Nye the Science Guy: Climates.*
- ☐ *Bill Nye the Science Guy: Comets and Meteors.*
- ☐ *Bill Nye the Science Guy: Communication.*
- ☐ *Bill Nye the Science Guy: Computers.*
- ☐ *Bill Nye the Science Guy: Deserts.*
- ☐ *Bill Nye the Science Guy: Digestion.*
- ☐ *Bill Nye the Science Guy: Dinosaurs.*
- ☐ *Bill Nye the Science Guy: Do-It-Yourself Science.*
- ☐ *Bill Nye the Science Guy: Earth's Crust.*
- ☐ *Bill Nye the Science Guy: Earth's Seasons.*
- ☐ *Bill Nye the Science Guy: Earthquakes.*
- ☐ *Bill Nye the Science Guy: Electrical Current.*
- ☐ *Bill Nye the Science Guy: Energy.*
- ☐ *Bill Nye the Science Guy: Erosion.*
- ☐ *Bill Nye the Science Guy: Evolution.*
- ☐ *Bill Nye the Science Guy: Eyeball.*
- ☐ *Bill Nye the Science Guy: Farming.*
- ☐ *Bill Nye the Science Guy: Fish.*
- ☐ *Bill Nye the Science Guy: Flight.*
- ☐ *Bill Nye the Science Guy: Flowers.*
- ☐ *Bill Nye the Science Guy: Fluids.*

- ☐ *Bill Nye the Science Guy: Food Web.*
- ☐ *Bill Nye the Science Guy: Forensics.*
- ☐ *Bill Nye the Science Guy: Forests.*
- ☐ *Bill Nye the Science Guy: Fossils.*
- ☐ *Bill Nye the Science Guy: Friction.*
- ☐ *Bill Nye the Science Guy: Garbage.*
- ☐ *Bill Nye the Science Guy: Genes.*
- ☐ *Bill Nye the Science Guy: Germs.*
- ☐ *Bill Nye the Science Guy: Gravity.*
- ☐ *Bill Nye the Science Guy: Heart.*
- ☐ *Bill Nye the Science Guy: Heat.*
- ☐ *Bill Nye the Science Guy: Human Transportation.*
- ☐ *Bill Nye the Science Guy: Insects.*
- ☐ *Bill Nye the Science Guy: Inventions.*
- ☐ *Bill Nye the Science Guy: Invertebrates.*
- ☐ *Bill Nye the Science Guy: Lakes and Ponds.*
- ☐ *Bill Nye the Science Guy: Life Cycles.*
- ☐ *Bill Nye the Science Guy: Light and Color.*
- ☐ *Bill Nye the Science Guy: Light Optics.*
- ☐ *Bill Nye the Science Guy: Magnetism.*
- ☐ *Bill Nye the Science Guy: Mammals.*
- ☐ *Bill Nye the Science Guy: Marine Mammals.*
- ☐ *Bill Nye the Science Guy: Measurement.*
- ☐ *Bill Nye the Science Guy: Momentum.*
- ☐ *Bill Nye the Science Guy: Motion.*
- ☐ *Bill Nye the Science Guy: Nutrition.*
- ☐ *Bill Nye the Science Guy: Ocean Exploration.*
- ☐ *Bill Nye the Science Guy: Ocean Life.*
- ☐ *Bill Nye the Science Guy: Oceanography.*
- ☐ *Bill Nye the Science Guy: Outer Space.*
- ☐ *Bill Nye the Science Guy: Patterns.*

- [ ] *Bill Nye the Science Guy: Phases of Matter.*
- [ ] *Bill Nye the Science Guy: Plants.*
- [ ] *Bill Nye the Science Guy: Pollution Solutions.*
- [ ] *Bill Nye the Science Guy: Populations.*
- [ ] *Bill Nye the Science Guy: Pressure.*
- [ ] *Bill Nye the Science Guy: Probability.*
- [ ] *Bill Nye the Science Guy: Pseudoscience.*
- [ ] *Bill Nye the Science Guy: Reptiles.*
- [ ] *Bill Nye the Science Guy: Respiration.*
- [ ] *Bill Nye the Science Guy: Rivers and Streams.*
- [ ] *Bill Nye the Science Guy: Rocks and Soil.*
- [ ] *Bill Nye the Science Guy: Science of Music.*
- [ ] *Bill Nye the Science Guy: Simple Machines.*
- [ ] *Bill Nye the Science Guy: Skin.*
- [ ] *Bill Nye the Science Guy: Smell.*
- [ ] *Bill Nye the Science Guy: Sound.*
- [ ] *Bill Nye the Science Guy: Space Exploration.*
- [ ] *Bill Nye the Science Guy: Spiders.*
- [ ] *Bill Nye the Science Guy: Spinning Things.*
- [ ] *Bill Nye the Science Guy: Static Electricity.*
- [ ] *Bill Nye the Science Guy: Storms.*
- [ ] *Bill Nye the Science Guy: The Moon.*
- [ ] *Bill Nye the Science Guy: The Planets.*
- [ ] *Bill Nye the Science Guy: The Sun.*
- [ ] *Bill Nye the Science Guy: Time.*
- [ ] *Bill Nye the Science Guy: Volcanoes.*
- [ ] *Bill Nye the Science Guy: Water Cycle.*
- [ ] *Bill Nye the Science Guy: Waves.*
- [ ] *Bill Nye the Science Guy: Wetlands.*
- [ ] *Bill Nye the Science Guy: Wind.*

DK Eyewitness Videos

- [ ] *Eyewitness: Amphibian*
- [ ] *Eyewitness: Ape*
- [ ] *Eyewitness: Arctic and Antarctic*
- [ ] *Eyewitness: Bear*
- [ ] *Eyewitness: Bird*
- [ ] *Eyewitness: Butterfly and Moth*
- [ ] *Eyewitness: Cat*
- [ ] *Eyewitness: Dinosaur*
- [ ] *Eyewitness: Dog*
- [ ] *Eyewitness: Fish*
- [ ] *Eyewitness: Flight*
- [ ] *Eyewitness: Horse*
- [ ] *Eyewitness: Human Machine*
- [ ] *Eyewitness: Insect*
- [ ] *Eyewitness: Island*
- [ ] *Eyewitness: Jungle*
- [ ] *Eyewitness: Life*
- [ ] *Eyewitness: Mammal*
- [ ] *Eyewitness: Monster*
- [ ] *Eyewitness: Mountain*
- [ ] *Eyewitness: Natural Disasters*
- [ ] *Eyewitness: Ocean*
- [ ] *Eyewitness: Planets*
- [ ] *Eyewitness: Plant*
- [ ] *Eyewitness: Pond and River*
- [ ] *Eyewitness: Prehistoric Life*
- [ ] *Eyewitness: Reptile*
- [ ] *Eyewitness: Rock and Mineral*
- [ ] *Eyewitness: Seashore*

- ☐ *Eyewitness: Shark*
- ☐ *Eyewitness: Sight*
- ☐ *Eyewitness: Skeleton*
- ☐ *Eyewitness: Survival*
- ☐ *Eyewitness: Volcano*
- ☐ *Eyewitness: Weather*

Mythbusters (arranged in order of production)

- ☐ *Mythbusters (Season 1): Jet-Assissted Chevy*
- ☐ *Mythbusters (Season 1): Biscuit Bazooka*
- ☐ *Mythbusters (Season 1): Poppy Seed Drug Test*
- ☐ *Mythbusters (Season 2): Exploding Toilet*
- ☐ *Mythbusters (Season 2): Cell Phone Destroys Gas Station*
- ☐ *Mythbusters (Season 2): Barrel of Bricks*
- ☐ *Mythbusters (Season 2): Penny Drop*
- ☐ *Mythbusters (Season 2): Buried Alive*
- ☐ *Mythbusters (Season 2): Lightning Strikes/tongue Piercing*
- ☐ *Mythbusters (Season 2): Stinky Car*
- ☐ *Mythbusters (Season 2): Alcatraz Escape*
- ☐ *Mythbusters (Season 2): Chicken Gun*
- ☐ *Mythbusters (Season 2): Explosive Decompression*
- ☐ *Mythbusters (Season 2): Sinking Titanic*
- ☐ *Mythbusters (Season 2): Breakstep Bridge*
- ☐ *Mythbusters (Season 2): Buried in Concrete*
- ☐ *Mythbusters (Season 3): Myths Revisited*
- ☐ *Mythbusters (Season 3): Scuba Diver and Car Capers*
- ☐ *Mythbusters (Season 3): Ancient Death Ray*
- ☐ *Mythbusters (Season 3): Elevator of Death*
- ☐ *Mythbusters (Season 3): Beat the Radar Dectector*
- ☐ *Mythbusters (Season 3): Quicksand*

- [ ] *Mythbusters (Season 3): Exploding Jawbreaker*
- [ ] *Mythbusters (Season 3): Ping Pong Rescue*
- [ ] *Mythbusters (Season 3): Boom Lift Catapult*
- [ ] *Mythbusters (Season 3): Exploding House*
- [ ] *Mythbusters (Season 3): Ming Dynasty Astronaut*
- [ ] *Mythbusters (Season 3): Brown Note*
- [ ] *Mythbusters (Season 3): Salsa Escape*
- [ ] *Mythbusters (Season 3): Exploding Port-a-Potty*
- [ ] *Mythbusters (Season 3): Is Yawning Contagious*
- [ ] *Mythbusters (Season 3): Cooling a Six-Pack*
- [ ] *Mythbusters (Season 3): Son of a Gun*
- [ ] *Mythbusters (Season 3): Breaking Glass*
- [ ] *Mythbusters (Season 3): Jet Pack*
- [ ] *Mythbusters (Season 3): Killer Brace Position*
- [ ] *Mythbusters (Season 3): Bullet-Proof Water*
- [ ] *Mythbusters (Season 3): Border Slingshot*
- [ ] *Mythbusters (Season 3): Killer Tissue Box*
- [ ] *Mythbusters (Season 3): Escape Slide-Parachute*
- [ ] *Mythbusters (Season 3): Mythbusters Revisited*
- [ ] *Mythbusters (Season 3): Chinese Invasion Alarm*
- [ ] *Mythbusters (Season 3): Mythbusters Revealed*
- [ ] *Mythbusters (Season 4): Killer Whirlpool*
- [ ] *Mythbusters (Season 4): Crimes and Myth-demeanors I*
- [ ] *Mythbusters (Season 4): Crimes and Myth-demeanors II*
- [ ] *Mythbusters (Season 4): Deadly Straw*
- [ ] *Mythbusters (Season 4): Earthquake Machine*
- [ ] *Mythbusters (Season 4): Diet Coke and Mentos*
- [ ] *Mythbusters (Season 4): Killer Cable Snaps*
- [ ] *Mythbusters (Season 4): Concrete Glider*
- [ ] *Mythbusters (Season 4): Air Cylinder Rocket*
- [ ] *Mythbusters (Season 4): More Myths Revisited*

- ☐ *Mythbusters (Season 4): Exploding Lighter*
- ☐ *Mythbusters (Season 4): Anti-Gravity Device*
- ☐ *Mythbusters (Season 4): Firearms Folklore*
- ☐ *Mythbusters (Season 4): 22,000 Foot Fall*
- ☐ *Mythbusters (Season 4): Shop 'Til You Drop*
- ☐ *Mythbusters (Season 4): Hollywood on Trial*
- ☐ *Mythbusters (Season 5): Holiday Special*
- ☐ *Mythbusters (Season 5): Pirate Special*
- ☐ *Mythbusters (Season 5): Hindenburg Mystery*
- ☐ *Mythbusters (Season 5): Underwater Car Escape*
- ☐ *Mythbusters (Season 5): Speed Cameras*
- ☐ *Mythbusters (Season 5): Dog Myths*
- ☐ *Mythbusters (Season 5): More Myths Reopened*
- ☐ *Mythbusters (Season 5): Voice Flame Extinguisher*
- ☐ *Mythbusters (Season 5): Birds in a Truck*
- ☐ *Mythbusters (Season 5): Walking on Water*
- ☐ *Mythbusters (Season 5): Western Myths*
- ☐ *Mythbusters (Season 5): Big Rig Myths*
- ☐ *Mythbusters (Season 5): Snow Special*
- ☐ *Mythbusters (Season 5): Grenades and Guts*
- ☐ *Mythbusters (Season 5): Baseball Myths*
- ☐ *Mythbusters (Season 5): Viewer Special*
- ☐ *Mythbusters (Season 5): Superhero Spcial*
- ☐ *Mythbusters (Season 5): Red Rag to a Bull*
- ☐ *Mythbusters (Season 5): Myth Revolution*
- ☐ *Mythbusters (Season 5): Trail Blazers*
- ☐ *Mythbusters (Season 5): Exploding Water Heater*
- ☐ *Mythbusters (Season 5): Idioms*
- ☐ *Mythbusters (Season 5): Pirates 2!*
- ☐ *Mythbusters (Season 5): Confederate Cannon*
- ☐ *Mythbusters (Season 5): Airplane Hour*

- [ ] *Mythbusters (Season 5): Episode 95*
- [ ] *Mythbusters (Season 5): Episode 96*
- [ ] *Mythbusters (Season 5): Episode 97*
- [ ] *Mythbusters (Season 5): Episode 98*
- [ ] *Mythbusters (Season 5): Viewers Special 2*
- [ ] *Mythbusters (Season 5): MacGyver Myths*
- [ ] *Mythbusters (Season 6): Alaska Special*
- [ ] *Mythbusters (Season 6): NASA Moon Landing*
- [ ] *Mythbusters (Season 6): Exploding Steak*
- [ ] *Mythbusters (Season 6): Ninjas 2*
- [ ] *Mythbusters (Season 6): Blind Driving*
- [ ] *Mythbusters (Season 6): Viral Hour*
- [ ] *Mythbusters (Season 6): Phone Book Friction*
- [ ] *Mythbusters (Season 6): Water Stun Gun*
- [ ] *Mythbusters (Season 6): Alcohol Myths*
- [ ] *Mythbusters (Season 6): Motorcycle Flip*
- [ ] *Mythbusters (Season 6): Coffin Punch*
- [ ] *Mythbusters (Season 6): End With a Bang*
- [ ] *Mythbusters (Season 6): Viewer Special Threequel*
- [ ] *Mythbusters (Season 7): Demolition Derby Special*
- [ ] *Mythbusters (Season 7): Alaska 2 Special*
- [ ] *Mythbusters (Season 7): Banana Slip Double Dip*
- [ ] *Mythbusters (Season 7): YouTube Special*
- [ ] *Mythbusters (Season 7): Swimming in Syrup*
- [ ] *Mythbusters (Season 7): Exploding Bumper*
- [ ] *Mythbusters (Season 7): Seesaw Saga*
- [ ] *Mythbusters (Season 7): Thermite vs. Ice*
- [ ] *Mythbusters (Season 7): Prison Escape*
- [ ] *Mythbusters (Season 7): Curving Bullets*
- [ ] *Mythbusters (Season 7): Car vs. Rain*
- [ ] *Mythbusters (Season 7): Knock Your Socks Off*

- [ ] *Mythbusters (Season 7): Duct Tape Hour*
- [ ] *Mythbusters (Season 7): Dirty vs. Clean Car*
- [ ] *Mythbusters (Season 7): Greased LIghtening*
- [ ] *Mythbusters (Season 7): Hurricane Windows*
- [ ] *Mythbusters (Season 7): Crash and Burn*
- [ ] *Mythbusters (Season 7): Myth Evolution*
- [ ] *Mythbusters (Season 7): Dumpster Diving*
- [ ] *Mythbusters (Season 7): Antacid Jail Break*
- [ ] *Mythbusters (Season 7): Unarmed and Unharmed*
- [ ] *Mythbusters (Season 7): Hidden Nasties*
- [ ] *Mythbusters (Season 7): Mini Myth Mahem*
- [ ] *Mythbusters (Season 7): Boomerang Bullet*
- [ ] *Mythbusters (Season 8): Soda Cup Killer*
- [ ] *Mythbusters (Season 8): Dive to Survive*
- [ ] *Mythbusters (Season 8): spy Car Escape*
- [ ] *Mythbusters (Season 8): Bottle Bash*
- [ ] *Mythbusters (Season 8): No Pain, No Gain*
- [ ] *Mythbusters (Season 8): Mythssion Control*
- [ ] *Mythbusters (Season 8): Duct Tape Hour 2*
- [ ] *Mythbusters (Season 8): Waterslide Wipeout*
- [ ] *Mythbusters (Season 8): Fireball StunGun*
- [ ] *Mythbusters (Season 8): Flu Fiction*
- [ ] *Mythbusters (Season 9): Hair of the Dog*
- [ ] *Mythbusters (Season 9): Storm Chasing Myths*
- [ ] *Mythbusters (Season 9): Cold Feet*
- [ ] *Mythbusters (Season 9): Table Cloth Chaos*
- [ ] *Mythbusters (Season 9): Arrow Machine Gun*
- [ ] *Mythbusters (Season 9): Mini Myth Madness*
- [ ] *Mythbusters (Season 9): Reverse Engineering*
- [ ] *Mythbusters (Season 9): Inverted Underwater Car*
- [ ] *Mythbusters (Season 9): Bug Special*

☐ *Mythbusters (Season 9): President's Challenge*

☐ *Mythbusters (Season 9): Green Hornet Special*

☐ *Mythbusters (Season 9): Operation Valkyrie*

☐ *Mythbusters (Season 10): Mission Impossible Mask*

☐ *Mythbusters (Season 10): Blue Ice*

☐ *Mythbusters (Season 10): Running on Water*

☐ *Mythbusters (Season 10): Bubble Trouble*

☐ *Mythbusters (Season 10): Torpedo Tastic*

☐ *Mythbusters (Season 10): Blow Your Own Sail*

☐ *Mythbusters (Season 10): Spy Car 2*

☐ *Mythbusters (Season 10): Dodge a Bullet*

☐ *Mythbusters (Season 10): Fixing a Flat*

☐ *Mythbusters (Season 10): Let There Be Light*

☐ *Mythbusters (Season 10): Paper Armor*

☐ *Mythbusters (Season 10): Planes, Trains, & Automobiles*

☐ *Mythbusters (Season 11): Bikes and Bazookas*

☐ *Mythbusters (Season 11): Newton's Crane Cradle*

☐ *Mythbusters (Season 11): Walkk A Straight Line*

☐ *Mythbusters (Season 11): Duct Tape Plane*

☐ *Mythbusters (Season 11): Flying Guillotine*

☐ *Mythbusters (Season 11): Drain Disaster*

☐ *Mythbusters (Season 11): Wheel of Mythfortune*

☐ *Mythbusters (Season 11): Toilet Bomb*

☐ *Mythbusters (Season 11): Location, Location, Location*

☐ *Mythbusters (Season 11): Wet and Wild*

☐ *Mythbusters (Season 12): Duct Tape Island*

☐ *Mythbusters (Season 12): Fire vs. Ice*

☐ *Mythbusters (Season 12): Square Wheels*

☐ *Mythbusters (Season 12): Swinging Pirates*

☐ *Mythbusters (Season 12): Battle of the Sexes*

☐ *Mythbusters (Season 12): Driving in Heels*

☐ *Mythbusters (Season 12): Revenge of the Myth*

☐ *Mythbusters (Season 12): Bouncing Bullet*

☐ *Mythbusters (Season 12): Mailbag Special*

☐ *Mythbusters (Season 12): Bubble Pack Plunge*

☐ *Mythbusters (Season 12): Duel Dilemmas*

☐ *Mythbusters (Season 12): Hollywood Gunslingers*

☐ *Mythbusters (Season 13): Titanic Survival*

☐ *Mythbusters (Season 13): Trench Torpedo*

☐ *Mythbusters (Season 13): Hail Hijinx*

☐ *Mythbusters (Season 13): Fright Night*

☐ *Mythbusters (Season 13): Mini Myth Medley*

☐ *Mythbusters (Season 13): Cannonball Chemistry*

☐ *Mythbusters (Season 13): Food Fables*

☐ *Mythbusters (Season 13): Explosions A-Z*

☐ *Mythbusters (Season 14): JATO Rocket Car: Mission Accomplished?*

☐ *Mythbusters (Season 14): Deadliest Catch Crabtastic Special*

☐ *Mythbusters (Season 14): Down and Dirty/Earthquake Survival*

☐ *Mythbusters (Season 14): Indy Car Special*

☐ *Mythbusters (Season 14): Battle of the Sexes - Round 2*

☐ *Mythbusters (Season 14): Motorcycle Water Ski*

☐ *Mythbusters (Season 14): Hypermilling/Crash Cushions*

☐ *Mythbusters (Season 14): Duct Tape Canyon*

☐ *Mythbusters (Season 14): Painting with Explosives/Bifurcated Boat*

Real History Books

History Books for K-3rd Grades

General History Books (K-3rd Grades)

Ancient History (K-3rd Grades)

- ☐ Bailey, Linda. *Adventures in Ancient China (Good Times Travel Agency)*. ISBN 1550745484
- ☐ Bailey, Linda. *Adventures in Ancient Egypt (Good Times Travel Agency)*. ISBN 1550745484
- ☐ Bailey, Linda. *Adventures in Ancient Greece (Good Times Travel Agency)*. ISBN 1550745360
- ☐ Bailey, Linda. *Adventures in the Ice Age (Good Times Travel Agency)*. ISBN 1553375041
- ☐ Brett, Jan. *The First Dog*. ISBN 0152276513
- ☐ Cole, Joanna. *Ms. Frizzle's Adventures: Ancient Egypt*. ISBN
- ☐ Dubowski, Mark. *Discovery in the Cave (Step into Reading)*.
- ☐ Dubowski, Mark. *Ice Mummy (Step into Reading)*.
- ☐ Gauch, Sarah. *Voyage to the Pharos*.
- ☐ Greenburg, J.C. *In the Ice Age (Andrew Lost #12)*.
- ☐ Lasky, Kathryn. *The Librarian Who Measured the Earth*.
- ☐ McCully, Emily Arnold. *The Secret Cave: Discovering Lascaux*.
- ☐ Morley, Jacqueline. *You Wouldn't Want to Work on the Great Wall of China! Defenses You'd Rather not Build*.
- ☐ O'Connor, Jane. *Hidden Army: Clay soldiers of Ancient China (All Aboard Reading)*.
- ☐ Osborne, Mary Pope. *Day Of The Dragon-King (Magic Tree House 14)*. ISBN 0679890513

- ☐ Osborne, Mary Pope. *Hour of the Olympics (Magic Tree House No. 16)*. ISBN 0679890629
- ☐ Osborne, Mary Pope. *Mummies in the Morning (Magic Tree House, No. 3)*.
- ☐ Osborne, Mary Pope. *Sunset of the Sabertooth*. ISBN 0679863737
- ☐ Osborne, Mary Pope. *Vacation Under the Volcano (Magic Tree House, No. 13)*.
- ☐ Pilegard, Virginia. The *Emperor's Army: A Mathematical Adventure*.
- ☐ Platt, Richard. *Roman Diary: The Journal of Iliona of Mytilini: Captured and Sold as a Slave in Rome - AD 107*.
- ☐ Scieszka, Jon. *It's All Greek to Me #8 (Time Warp Trio)*.
- ☐ Scieszka, Jon. *See You Later, Gladiator #9 (Time Warp Trio)*.
- ☐ Scieszka, Jon. *Tut, Tut #6 (Time Warp Trio)*.

Medieval/Renaissance History Books (K-3rd Grades)

- ☐ Bailey, Linda. *Adventures in the Middle Ages (Good Times Travel Agency)*. ISBN 1550745409
- ☐ Bailey, Linda. *Adventures With the Vikings (Good Times Travel Agency)*. ISBN 1550745441
- ☐ Brown, Don. *Across a Dark and Wild Sea*. ISBN 0761315349
- ☐ Daulaire, Ingri. *Leif the Lucky*. ISBN 0964380307
- ☐ De Angeli, Marguerite. *The Door in the Wall (Books for Young Readers)*. ISBN 0440227798
- ☐ Demi. *Genghis Khan*. ISBN 0761455477
- ☐ Engle, Margarita. *Summer Birds: The Butterflies of Maria Merian*.
- ☐ Fisher, Leonard Everett. *The Great Wall Of China*. ISBN 0689801785
- ☐ Hodges, Margaret. *the Kitchen Knight: A Tale of King Arthur*. ISBN 0823410633
- ☐ Krebs, Laurie. *We're Riding on a Caravan*. ISBN 184686108X
- ☐ Lattimore, Deborah Nourse. *The Sailor Who Captured the Sea: A Story of the Book of Kells*. ISBN 0064433420
- ☐ Maisner, Heather. *Diary of a Princess: A Tale from Marco Polo's Travels*. ISBN 1422353028

- [ ] Osborne, Mary Pope. *Monday with a Mad Genius (Magic Tree House, No. 38).* ISBN 0375837302

- [ ] Platt, Richard. *Castle Diary: The Journal of Tobias Burgess.* ISBN 0763621641

- [ ] Platt, Richard. *Pirate Diary: The Journal of Jake Carpenter.* ISBN 0763628654

- [ ] Rhoads, Dorothy. *The Corn Grows Ripe.* ISBN 0140363130

- [ ] Robertson, Bruce. *Marguerite Makes a Book.* ISBN 089236372X

- [ ] Rumford, James. *From the Good Mountain: How Gutenberg Changed the World.*

- [ ] Scieszka, Jon. *The Knights of the Kitchen Table #1 (Time Warp Trio).* ISBN 0142400432

- [ ] Scieszka, Jon. *Sam Samurai #10 (Time Warp Trio).* ISBN 0142400882

- [ ] Scieszka, Jon. *Me Oh Maya #13 (Time Warp Trio).* ISBN 0142403008

- [ ] Scieszka, Jon. *Da Wild, Da Crazy, Da Vinci #14 (Time Warp Trio).* ISBN 0142404659

- [ ] Scieszka, Jon. *Marco? Polo! #16 (Time Warp Trio).* ISBN 0142411779

- [ ] Scieszka, Jon. *Time Warp Trio: You Can't, but Genghis Khan (Time Warp Trio).* ISBN 0142411779

- [ ] Wisniewski, David. *Sundiata: Lion King of Mali.* ISBN 0395764815

Early Modern History Books (K-3rd Grades)

- [ ] Adler, David A. *A Picture Book of Florence Nightengale.*

- [ ] Adler, David A. *A Picture Book of Frederick Douglass.*

- [ ] Adler, David A. *A Picture Book of Harriet Tubman.*

- [ ] Adler, David A. *A Picture Book of Simon Bolivar.*

- [ ] Adler, David A. *A Picture Book of Sojourner Truth.*

- [ ] Brighton, Catherine. *My Napoleon.*

- [ ] Brown, Don. *Rare Treasure: Mary Anning and Her Remarkable Discoveries.*

- [ ] D'Aulaire, Ingri and Edgar. *Columbus.*

- [ ] Gerrard, Roy. *Sir Francis Drake and His Daring Deeds.*

- [ ] Osborne, Mary Pope. *A Crazy Day with Cobras.*

- [ ] Scieszka, Jon. *Sam Samurai #10 (Time Warp Trio).* ISBN 0142400882

- ☐ Schanzer, Rosalyn. *How We Crossed The West: The Adventures Of Lewis And Clark.*
- ☐ Stanley, Diane. *Shaka: King of the Zulus.*

Modern History (K-3rd Grades)

World War I

- ☐ Hopkinson, Deborah. *Knit Your Bit: A World War I Story.*

World War II

- ☐ Adler, David A. *A Picture Book of Anne Frank.*
- ☐ Borden, Louise. *The Greatest Skating Race: A World War II Story from the Netherlands.*
- ☐ Borden, Louise. *The LIttle Ships: The Heroic Rescue at Dunkirk.*
- ☐ Hesse, Karen. *The Cats in Krasinkski Square.*
- ☐ Hoestlandt, Jo. *Star of Fear, Star of Hope.*
- ☐ Hunter, Sara Hoagland. *The Unbreakable Code.*
- ☐ Littlesugar, Amy. *Willy and Max: A Holocaust Story.*
- ☐ Mochizuki, Ken. *Baseball Saved Us.* Japanese internment camps.
- ☐ Raven, Margot Theis. *Mercedes and the Chocolate Pilot.*
- ☐ Russo, Marisabina. *Always Remember Me: How One Family Survived World War II.*
- ☐ Selbert, Kathryn. *War Dogs: Churchill and Rufus.*
- ☐ Tryszynska-Frederick. *Luba: The Angel of Bergen-Belsen.*
- ☐ Tunnell, Michael O. *Candy Bomber: The Story of the Berlin Airlift's "Chocolate Pilot."*
- ☐ Uchida, Yoshiko. *The Bracelet.* Japanese internment.
- ☐ Wilbur, Helen. *Lily's Victory Garden.*
- ☐ Wiviott, Meg. *Benno and the Night of Broken Glass.*

Russia under Stalin

- ☐ Yelchin, Eugene. *Breaking Stalin's Nose.*

Chinese Cultural Revolution

- [ ] Hong, Chen Jiang. *Mao and Me.*
- [ ] Jiang, Ji-li. *Red Kte, Blue Kite.*

Korean War

- [ ] Balgassi, Haemi. *Peacebound Trains.*

Cuban Revolution

- [ ] Colon, Edie. *Good-bye, Havana! Hola, New York!.*
- [ ] Wells, Rosemary. *My Havanna.*

Space Race

- [ ] Brown, Don. *One Giant Leap: The Story of Neil Armstrong.*

Vietnam War

- [ ] Bunting, Eve. *The Wall (Reading Rainbow Books).*
- [ ] Garland, Sherry. *The Lotus Seed.*
- [ ] Myers, Walter Dean. *Patrol: An American Soldier in Vietnam.*

Cambodia, Khmer Rouge Regime

- [ ] O'Brien, Anne Sibley. *A Path of Stars.*

War in Afghanistan

- [ ] Mortenson, Greg. *Listen to the Wind: The Story of Dr. Greg & Three Cups of Tea.*
- [ ] Williams, Karen Lynn. *Four Feet, Two Sandals.*
- [ ] Winter, Jeanette. *Nasreen's Secret School.*

Iraq War

- [ ] Ellis, Deborah. *Children of War: Voices of Iraqi Refugees.*
- [ ] Ellis, Deborah. *No Safe Place.* Iraqi War, human trafficking.
- [ ] Rumford, James. *Silent Music: A Story of Bagdad.*

☐ Winter, Jeanette. *The Librarian of Basra.*

Sudan Civil War

☐ Williams, Mary. *Brothers in Hope: The Story of the Lost Boys of Sudan.*

Miscellaneous

☐ Brown, Don. *All Stations! Distress! (Actual Times).* The sinking of the Titanic

☐ Brown, Don. *A Voice from the Wilderness.* Women's right to vote

☐ KamKwamba, William. *The Boy Who Harnessed the Wind: Young Reader's Edition.*

☐ Milway, Katie Smith. *The Good Garden: How One Family Went from Hunger to Having Enough.*

☐ Milway, Katie Smith. *One Hen: How One Small Loan Made a Big Difference.*

United States History (K-3rd Grades)

General United States History Books (K-3rd Grades)

☐ Adler, David A. *A Picture Book of Cesar Chavez.*

☐ Adler, David A. *A Picture Book of Frederick Douglass.*

☐ Adler, David A. *A Picture Book of Harriet Tubman.*

☐ Adler, David A. *A Picture Book of Martin Luther King Jr.*

☐ Adler, David A. *A Picture Book of Rosa Parks.*

☐ Adler, David A. *A Picture Book of Sojourner Truth.*

☐ Benchley, Nathaniel. *George the Drummer Boy (I Can Read Book).*

☐ Benchley, Nathaniel. *Sam the Minuteman (I Can Read Book).*

☐ Brenner, Martha. *Abe Lincoln's Hat (Step into Reading).*

☐ Brown, Don. *Alice Ramsey's Grand Adventure.*

☐ Brown, Don. *Bright Path: Young Jim Thorpe.*

☐ Brown, Don. *Dolley Madison Saves George Washington.*

☐ Brown, Don. *Gold! Gold from the American River!: January 24, 1848: The Day the Gold Rush Began (Actual Times).*

- [ ] Brown, Don. *Henry and the Cannons: An Extraordinary True Story of the American Revolution.*
- [ ] Brown, Don. *One Giant Leap: The Story of Neil Armstrong.*
- [ ] Brown, Don. *Teedie: The Story of Young Teddy Roosevelt.*
- [ ] Bruchac, Joseph. *Squanto's Journey: The Story of the First Thanksgiving.*
- [ ] Bruchac, Joseph. *Trail of Tears (Step Into Reading).*
- [ ] Chandra, Deborah. *George Washington's Teeth.*
- [ ] Coerr, Eleanor. *Buffalo Bill and the Pony Express (I Can Read Book).*
- [ ] Corey, Shana. *Here Come the Girl Scouts!: The Amazing All-True Story of Juliette 'Daisy' Gordon Low and Her Great Adventure.*
- [ ] D'Aulaire, Ingri and Edgar. *Abraham Lincoln.*
- [ ] D'Aulaire, Ingri and Edgar. *Benjamin Franklin.*
- [ ] D'Aulaire, Ingri and Edgar. *Buffalo Bill.*
- [ ] D'Aulaire, Ingri and Edgar. *Columbus.*
- [ ] D'Aulaire, Ingri and Edgar. *George Washington.*
- [ ] D'Aulaire, Ingri and Edgar. *Leif the Lucky.*
- [ ] D'Aulaire, Ingri and Edgar. *Pocahontas.*
- [ ] Fraser, Mary Ann. *Ten Mile Day: And the Building of the Transcontinental Railroad.*
- [ ] Fritz, Jean. *George Washington's Breakfast.*
- [ ] Harness, Cheryl. *Amazing Impossible Erie Canal.*
- [ ] Harness, Cheryl. *They're Off!: The Story of the Pony Express.*
- [ ] Harness, Cheryl. *Three Young Pilgrims.*
- [ ] Jakes, John. *Susanna of the Alamo: A True Story.*
- [ ] Kay, Verla. *Gold Fever.*
- [ ] Keller, Laurie. *The Scrambled States of America.*
- [ ] Keller, Laurie. *The Scrambled States of America Talent Show.*
- [ ] Krensky, Stephen. *Davy Crockett: A Life on the Frontier.*
- [ ] Krensky, Stephen. *Pearl Harbor : Ready To Read Level 3.*
- [ ] Kulling, Monica. *Eat My Dust! Henry Ford's First Race (Step into Reading).*
- [ ] Kulling, Monica. *Francis Scott Key's Star-Spangled Banner (Step into Reading).*

- [ ] Kulling, Monica. *Listen Up!: Alexander Graham Bell's Talking Machine (Step into Reading)*.
- [ ] Lawson, Robert. *Ben and Me: An Astonishing Life of Benjamin Franklin by His Good Mouse Amos*.
- [ ] Lawson, Robert. *Mr. Revere and I: Being an Account of certain Episodes in the Career of Paul Revere,Esq. as Revealed by his Horse*.
- [ ] Levitin, Sonia. *Boom Town*.
- [ ] Levitin, Sonia. *Nine for California*.
- [ ] Lied, Kate. *Potato: A Tale From The Great Depression*.
- [ ] Limbaugh, Rush. *Rush Revere and the Brave Pilgrims: Time-Travel Adventures with Exceptional Americans*.
- [ ] Limbaugh, Rush. *Rush Revere and the First Patriots: Time-Travel Adventures With Exceptional Americans*.
- [ ] McCully, Emily Arnold. *The Escape of Oney Judge: Martha Washington's Slave Finds Freedom*.
- [ ] McKissack, Patricia C. *Goin' Someplace Special*. Segregated south.
- [ ] Monjo, F.N. *The Drinking Gourd: A Story of the Underground Railroad (I Can Read Book)*.
- [ ] Mora, Pat. *Tomas and the Library Lady (Dragonfly Books)*.
- [ ] Murphy, Frank. *Thomas Jefferson's Feast (Step into Reading)*.
- [ ] Osborne, Mary Pope. *Civil War on Sunday*.
- [ ] Osborne, Mary Pope. *Revolutionary War on Wednesday (Magic Tree House #22)*.
- [ ] Rappaport, Doreen. *Martin's Big Words: The Life of Dr. Martin Luther King, Jr.*
- [ ] Redmond, Shirley Raye. *Lewis and Clark: A Prairie Dog for the President*.
- [ ] Reich, Susanna. *Minette's Feast: The Delicious Story of Julia Child and Her Cat*.
- [ ] Rockwell, Anne. *Only Passing Through*.
- [ ] Sandin, Joan. *The Long Way to a New Land (I Can Read Book)*.
- [ ] Sandin, Joan. *The Long Way Westward (I Can Read Book)*.
- [ ] Schanzer, Rosalyn. *How We Crossed The West: The Adventures Of Lewis And Clark*.

- ☐ Schroeder, Alan. *Minty: A Story of Young Harriet Tubman.*
- ☐ Scieszka, Jon. *Hey Kid, Want to Buy a Bridge? #11 (Time Warp Trio).* ISBN 0142400890
- ☐ Scieszka, Jon. *Oh Say, I Can't See #15 (Time Warp Trio).* ISBN 0142408085
- ☐ Sewall, Marcia. *The Pilgrims of Plymoth.*
- ☐ Shea, George. *First Flight: The Story of Tom Tate and the Wright Brothers (I Can Read Book).*
- ☐ Stanley, Diane. *Joining the Boston Tea Party (The Time-Traveling Twins).*
- ☐ Stanley, Diane. *Roughing It on the Oregon Trail (The Time-Traveling Twins).*
- ☐ Stanley, Diane. *Thanksgiving on Plymouth Plantation (The Time-Traveling Twins).*
- ☐ Stemple, Heidi E. *Roanoke: The Lost Colony--An Unsolved Mystery from History.*
- ☐ St. George, Judith. *The Journey of the One and Only Declaration of Independence.*
- ☐ Turner, Ann. *Dust for Dinner (I Can Read Book - Level 3).*
- ☐ Weatherford, Carole Boston. *Dear Mr. Rosenwald.* Rya, Pam Muñoz. *Amelia and Eleanor Go for a Ride.*
- ☐ Weatherford, Carole Boston. *Freedom on the Menu: The Greensboro Sit-Ins.*
- ☐ Weatherford, Carole Boston. *Moses: When Harriet Tubman Led Her People to Freedom.*
- ☐ Wiles, Deborah. *Freedom Summer.*
- ☐ Winter, Jeanette. *Follow the Drinking Gourd.*
- ☐ Winter, Jonah. *Born and Bred in the Great Depression.*
- ☐ Yin. *Coolies.*

Series of United States History Books (K-3rd Grades)

<u>**My America**</u> (in chronological order)

- ☐ Gregory, Kristiana. *My America: Five Smooth Stones: Hope's Revolutionary War Diary, Book One.*

☐ Gregory, Kristiana. *My America: We Are Patriots: Hope's Revolutionary War Diary, Book Two.* Hermes, Patricia. *My America: Our Strange New Land: Elizabeth's Jamestown Colony Diary, Book One.*

☐ Hermes, Patricia. *My America: The Starving Time: Elizabeth's Jamestown Colony Diary, Book Two.*

☐ Hermes, Patricia. *My America: Season of Promise: Elizabeth's Jamestown Colony Diary, Book Three.*

☐ Hermes, Patricia. *My America: Westward To Home: Joshua's Oregon Trail Diary, Book One.*

☐ Hermes, Patricia. *My America: A Perfect Place: Joshua's Oregon Trail Diary, Book Two.*

☐ Hermes, Patricia. *My America: The Wild Year: Joshua's Oregon Trail Diary, Book Three.*

☐ McMullan, Kate. *My America: As Far As I Can See: Meg's Prairie Diary, Book One.*

☐ McMullan, Kate. *My America: For This Land: Meg's Prairie Diary, Book Two.*

☐ McMullan, Kate. *My America: A Fine Start: Meg's Prairie Diary, Book Three.*

☐ Osborne, Mary Pope. *My America: My Brother's Keeper: Virginia's Civil War Diary, Book One.*

☐ Osborne, Mary Pope. *My America: After the Rain: Virginia's Civil War Diary, Book Two.*

☐ Osborne, Mary Pope. *My America: A Time To Dance: Virginia's Civil War Diary, Book Three.*

☐ Osborne, Mary Pope. *Civil War On Sunday (Magic Tree House #21).* ISBN 067989067X

☐ Osborne, Mary Pope. *Buffalo Before Breakfast (Magic Tree House #18).* ISBN 0679890645

☐ Osborne, Mary Pope. *Tonight on the Titanic (Magic Tree House, No. 17).* ISBN 0679890637

☐ Wyeth, Sharon Dennis. *My America: Freedom's Wings: Corey's Underground Railroad Diary, Book One.*

- ☐ Wyeth, Sharon Dennis. *My America: Flying Free: Corey's Underground Railroad Diary, Book Two.*
- ☐ Wyeth, Sharon Dennis. *My America: Message In The Sky: Corey's Underground Railroad Diary, Book Three.*

Magic Tree House (in chronological order)
- ☐ Osborne, Mary Pope. *Thanksgiving on Thursday (Magic Tree House #27).* ISBN 0375806156
- ☐ Osborne, Mary Pope. *Revolutionary War on Wednesday (Magic Tree House #22).* ISBN 0679890688

History Books for 4th-8th Grades

General History Books (4th-8th Grades)

Ancient History

Ice Age
- ☐ Bailey, Linda. *Adventures in the Ice Age (Good Times Travel Agency).* ISBN 1553375041
- ☐ Cowley, Marjorie. *Dar and the Spearthrower.*
- ☐ Deary, Terry. *Savage Stone Age.*
- ☐ Denzel, Justen. *The Boy of the Painted Cave.*
- ☐ Fleming, Fergus. *Stone Age Sentinel.*
- ☐ Malam, John. *You Wouldn't Want to Be a Mammoth Hunter!: Dangerous Beasts You'd Rather Not Encounter.* ISBN 0531163970

Ancient Mesopotamia
- ☐ Morley, Jacqueline. *You Wouldn't Want to Be a Sumerian Slave!: A Life of Hard Labor You'd Rather Avoid.* ISBN
- ☐ Matthews, Rupert. *You Wouldn't Want to Be an Assyrian Soldier!: An Ancient Army You'd Rather Not Join.* ISBN 0531189228
- ☐ Wilson, Diane. *To Ride the God's Own Stallion.*

☐ Williamson, Joanne. *Hittite Warrior.*

Ancient Egypt

☐ Deary, Terry. *Awesome Egyptians (Horrible Histories).*

☐ Deary, Terry. *Awful Egyptians (Horrible Histories).*

☐ Friesner, Esther. *Sphinx's Princess.*

☐ Friesner, Esther. *Sphinx's Queen.* Gregory, Kristiana. *Cleopatra VII: Daughter of the Nile, Egypt, 57 B.C (The Royal Diaries).*

☐ McGraw, Eloise Jarvis. *The Golden Goblet.*

☐ Morley, Jacqueline. *You Wouldn't Want to Be a Pyramid Builder!: A Hazardous Job You'd Rather Not Have.*

☐ Norton, Andre. *Shadow Hawk.*

☐ Pipe, Jim. *You Wouldn't Want to Be Cleopatra!: An Egyptian Ruler You'd Rather Not Be.*

☐ Stanley, Diane. *Cleopatra.*

☐ Stewart, David. *You Wouldn't Want to Be an Egyptian Mummy!: Disgusting Things You'd Rather Not Know.*

☐ Stewart, David. *You Wouldn't Want to Be Tutankhamen!: A Mummy Who Really Got Meddled With.*

Ancient Greece

☐ Antram, David. *You Wouldn't Want to Be a Slave in Ancient Greece!: A Life You'd Rather Not Have.* ISBN 0750232544

☐ Bailey, Linda. *Adventures in Ancient Greece (Good Times Travel Agency).* ISBN 1550745360

☐ Bendick, Jeanne. *Archimedes and the Door of Science.*

☐ Deary, Terry. *Groovy Greeks (Horrible Histories).*

☐ Ford, Michael. *You Wouldn't Want to Be a Greek Athlete: Races You'd Rather Not Run.* ISBN 978-0531163948

☐ Lasky, Kathryn. *The LIbrarian Who Measured the Earth.*

- ☐ Morley, Jacqueline. *You Wouldn't Want To Be In Alexander The Great's Army!: Miles You'd Rather Not March.* ISBN 0531123901
- ☐ Roberts, Katherine. *I Am the Great Horse.*
- ☐ Wilhelm, Doug. *Alexander the Great: Master of the Ancient World.*

Ancient Rome

- ☐ Brooks, Philip. *Hannibal: Rome's Worst Nightmare (Wicked History).*
- ☐ Deary, Terry. *Rotten Romans (Horrible Histories).*
- ☐ Deary, Terry. *Ruthless Romans (Horrible Histories).*
- ☐ Demi. *The Legend of Saint Nicholas.*
- ☐ Malam, John. *You Wouldn't Want to Be a Roman Gladiator!: Gory Things You'd Rather Not Know.* ISBN 0531162044
- ☐ Malam, John. *You Wouldn't Want to Live in Pompeii! A Volcanic Eruption You'd Rather Avoid.* ISBN 0531169006
- ☐ Moss, Marissa. *Galen: My Life in Imperial Rome.*
- ☐ Price, Sean Stewart. *Attila the Hun: Leader of the Barbarian Hordes (Wicked History).*
- ☐ Rinaldo, Denise. *Julius Caesar: Dictator for Life (Wicked History).*
- ☐ Stewart, David. *You Wouldn't Want to Be a Roman Soldier!: Barbarians You'd Rather Not Meet.* ISBN 0531124487
- ☐ Sutcliff, Rosemary. *The Eagle of the Ninth (Roman Britain Trilogy, Book 1).*
- ☐ Sutcliff, Rosemary. *The Silver Branch (Roman Britain Trilogy, Book 2).*
- ☐ Sutcliff, Rosemary. *The Lantern Bearers (Roman Britain Trilogy, Book 3).*
- ☐ Sutcliff, Rosemary. *Outcast.*
- ☐ Winterfield, Henry. *Dectectives in Togas.*
- ☐ Winterfield, Henry. *Mystery of the Roman Ransom.*

Ancient China

- ☐ Morley, Jacqueline. *You Wouldn't Want to Work on the Great Wall of China!: Defenses You'd Rather Not Build.*

- ☐ Osborne, Mary Pope. *Day of the Dragon-King.*
- ☐ Yep, Lawrence. *Lady of Ch'iao Kuo: Warrior of the South, Southern China, 531 A.D (The Royal Diaries).*

Ancient India

- ☐ Demi. *The Fantastic Adventures of Krishna.*

Medieval/Renaissance (4th-8th Grades)

General Medieval/Renaissance History Books (4th-8th Grades)

- ☐ Alder, Elizabeth. *The King's Shadow.*
- ☐ Bailey, Linda. *Adventures with the Vikings.*
- ☐ Burns, Khephra. *Mansa Musa: The Lion of Mali.*
- ☐ Demi. *Genghis Khan.*
- ☐ Demi. *Muhammad.*
- ☐ Demi. *Rumi: Persian Poet, Whirling Dervish.*
- ☐ Diconsiglio, John. *Pizarro: Destroyer of the Inca Empire (Wicked History)*
- ☐ Ellis, Deborah. *A Company of Fools.*
- ☐ Fritz, Jean. *Brendan the Navigator.*
- ☐ Galloway, Priscilla. *Archers, Alchemists, and 98 Other Medieval Jobs You Might Have Loved or Loathed.*
- ☐ Goldberg, Enid A. *Tomas de Torquemada: Architect of Torture During the Spanish Inquisition (Wicked History).*
- ☐ Grant K.M. *Blaze of Silver (de Granville Trilogy).* King Richard's Return
- ☐ Grant, K.M. *Blood Red Horse (de Granville Trilogy).* King Richard's Crusade
- ☐ Grant, K.M. *Green Jasper (de Granville Trilogy).* King Richard's Imprisonment
- ☐ Gray, Elizabeth Janet. *Adam of the Road.*
- ☐ Koningsburg, E.L. *A Proud Taste for Scarlet and Miniver.*
- ☐ McGraw, Eloise Jarvis. *The Striped Ships.*
- ☐ Park, Linda Sue. *A Single Shard.*
- ☐ Phillips, Robin. *Who in the World Was the Acrobatic Empress?*
- ☐ Price, Sean. *Henry VIII: Royal Beheader. (Wicked History).*

- [ ] Price, Sean. *Ivan the Terrible: Tsar of Death (Wicked History).*
- [ ] Rumford, Jamaes. *Traveling Man: The Journey of Ibn Battuta 1325-1354.*
- [ ] Seredy, Kate. *The White Stag.*
- [ ] Stanley, Diane. *Joan of Arc.*
- [ ] Stanley, Diane. *Saladin: Noble Prince of Islam.*
- [ ] Walsh, Jill Paton. *The Emperor's Winding Sheet.*
- [ ] Willard, Barbara. *Augustine Came to Kent.*
- [ ] Willard, Barbara. *Son of Charlemagne.*

Series of Medieval/Renaissance History Books (4th-8th Grades)

You Wouldn't Want to Be . . .

- [ ] Graham, Ian. *You Wouldn't Want to Be Sir Isaac Newton!: A Lonely Life You'd Rather Not Lead* . ISBN 0531230406
- [ ] Hynson, Colin. *You Wouldn't Want to Be an Inca Mummy!: A One-Way Journey You'd Rather Not Make.* ISBN 0531139263
- [ ] Langley, Andrew. *You Wouldn't Want to Be a Viking Explorer!: Voyages You'd Rather Not Make.* ISBN 0531162052
- [ ] MacDonald, Fiona. *You Wouldn't Want to Be a Medieval Knight!: Armor You'd Rather Not Wear.* ISBN 0531163954
- [ ] MacDonald, Fiona. *You Wouldn't Want to Be a Crusader!: A War You'd Rather Not Fight.* ISBN 0531123928
- [ ] MacDonald, Fiona. *You Wouldn't Want to Be an Aztec Sacrifice! Gruesome Things You'd Rather Not Know.* ISBN 0531162095
- [ ] MacDonald, Fiona. *You Wouldn't Want to Be a Samurai!: A Deadly Career You'd Rather Not Pursue.* ISBN 0531205169
- [ ] MacDonald, Fiona. *You Wouldn't Want to Be in a Medieval Dungeon!: Prisoners You'd Rather Not Meet.* ISBN 0531245047
- [ ] Malam, John. *You Wouldn't Want to Be a Pirate's Prisoner!: Horrible Things You'd Rather Not Know.* ISBN 0531163687

☐ Malam, John. *You Wouldn't Want to Sail in the Spanish Armada!: An Invasion You'd Rather Not Launch.* ISBN 0531169995

☐ Matthews, Rupert. *You Wouldn't Want to Be a Mayan Soothsayer!: Fortunes You'd Rather Not Tell.* ISBN 0531139255

☐ Morley, Jacqueline. *You Wouldn't Want to Be a Shakespearean Actor!: Some Roles You Might Not Want to Play.* ISBN 0531228266

☐ Morley, Jacqueline. *You Wouldn't Want to Be in the Forbidden City!: A Sheltered Life You'd Rather Avoid.* ISBN 0531169014

☐ Morley, Jacqueline. *You Wouldn't Want to Explore with Marco Polo!: A Really Long Trip You'd Rather Not Take.* ISBN 0531205185

☐ Morley, Jacqueline. *You Wouldn't Want to Live in a Medieval Castle!: A Home You'd Rather Not Inhabit.* ISBN 0531219135

☐ MacDonald, Fiona. *You Wouldn't Want to Be Joan of Arc!: A Mission You Might Want to Miss.* ISBN 0531228282

☐ MacDonald, Fiona. *You Wouldn't Want to Be Married to Henry VIII! A Husband You'd Rather Not Have.* ISBN 0750235969

☐ MacDonald, Fiona. *You Wouldn't Want to Work on a Medieval Cathedral!: A Difficult Job That Never Ends.* ISBN 0531137848

☐ Morley, Jacqueline. *You Wouldn't Want to Work on the Great Wall of China!: Defenses You'd Rather Not Build.* ISBN 0531124495

☐ Salariya, David. *You Wouldn't Want to Be Mary, Queen of Scots!: A Ruler Who Really Lost Her Head.* ISBN 053114853X

☐ Senior, Kathryn. *You Wouldn't Want to Be Sick in the 16th Century!: Diseases You'd Rather Not Catch.* ISBN 0531163660

☐ Stewart, David. *You Wouldn't Want to Explore With Sir Francis Drake!: A Pirate You'd Rather Not Know.* ISBN 0531123936

The Royal Diaries

☐ Danticat, Edwidge. *Anacaona: Golden Flower, Haiti, 1490 (The Royal Diaries).*

☐ Gregory, Kristiana. *Eleanor: Crown Jewel of Aquitaine, France, 1136 (The Royal Diaries).*

- ☐ Holman, Sheri. *Sondok: Princess of the Moon and Stars, Korea, A.D. 595 (The Royal Diaries)*.
- ☐ Lasky, Kathryn. *Elizabeth I: Red Rose of the House of Tudor, England, 1544 (The Royal Diaries)*.
- ☐ Lasky, Kathryn. *Mary, Queen of Scots: Queen Without a Country, France, 1553 (The Royal Diaries)*.
- ☐ Meyer, Carolyn. *Isabel: Jewel of Castilla, Spain, 1466 (The Royal Diaries)*.

Horrible Histories

- ☐ Deary, Terry. *The Angry Aztecs (Horrible Histories)*.
- ☐ Deary, Terry. *The Cut-Throat Celts (Horrible Histories)*.
- ☐ Deary, Terry. *The Incredible Incas (Horrible Histories)*.
- ☐ Deary, Terry. *The Measly Middle Ages (Horrible Histories)*.
- ☐ Deary, Terry. *The Smashing Saxons (Horrible Histories)*.
- ☐ Deary, Terry. *The Stormin' Normans (Horrible Histories)*.
- ☐ Deary, Terry. *The Vicious Vikings (Horrible Histories)*.

Early Modern History Books (4th-8th Grades)

see also United States History

General Early Modern History Books (4th-8th Grades)

- ☐ Blackwood, Gary. *The Shakespeare Stealer*.
- ☐ Blackwood, Gary. *Shakespeare's Scribe*.
- ☐ Blackwood, Gary. *Shakespeare's Spy*.
- ☐ Heuston, Kimberley. *Napoleon: Emperor and Conqueror (Wicked History)*.
- ☐ Koningsburg, E.L. *The Second Mrs. Giaconda*.
- ☐ Nick, Charles. *Sir Francis Drake: Slave Trader and Pirate (Wicked History)*.
- ☐ Patterson, Katherine. *Rebels of the Heavenly Kingdom*. Taiping Rebellion, China
- ☐ Rabin, Staton. *Betsy and the Emperor*.
- ☐ Rumford, James. *Seeker of Knowledge: The Man Who Deciphered Egyptian Hieroglyphs*.

☐ Shearer, Robert G. *Famous Men of the Renaissance and Reformation.*

☐ Stanley, Diane. *Peter the Great.*

☐ Stanley, Diane. *Shaka: King of the Zulus.*

☐ Vennema, Peter. *Bard of Avon: The Story of William Shakespeare.*

Series of Early Modern History Books (4th-8th Grades)

You Wouldn't Want to Be . . .

☐ Bergin, Mark. *You Wouldn't Want to Travel with Captain Cook!: A Voyage You'd Rather Not Make.* ISBN 0531124460

☐ Cook, Peter. *You Wouldn't Want to Sail on a 19th-Century Whaling Ship!: Grisly Tasks You'd Rather Not Do.* ISBN 0531163997

☐ MacDonald, Fiona. *You Wouldn't Want to Be a Victorian Servant!: A Thankless Job You'd Rather Not Have.* ISBN 0531169979

☐ Malam, John. *You Wouldn't Want to Be a 19th-Century Coal Miner in England!: A Dangerous Job You'd Rather Not Have.* ISBN 0531169960

☐ Malam, John. *You Wouldn't Want to Be a Victorian Mill Worker!: A Grueling Job You'd Rather Not Have.* ISBN 053113928X

☐ Pipe, Jim. *You Wouldn't Want to Be an Aristocrat in the French Revolution!: A Horrible Time in Paris You'd Rather Avoid.* ISBN 0531139271

☐ Pipe, Jim. *You Wouldn't Want to Sail on an Irish Famine Ship!: A Trip Across the Atlantic You'd Rather Not Make.* ISBN 0531148548

The Royal Diaries

☐ Denenberg, Barry. *Elisabeth: The Princess Bride, Austria-Hungary, 1853 (The Royal Diaries).*

☐ Gregory, Kristiana. *Catherine: The Great Journey, Russia, 1743 (The Royal Diaries).*

☐ Kirwan, Anna. *Victoria: May Blossom of Britannia, England, 1829. (The Royal Diaries).*

- ☐ Lasky, Kathryn. *Jahanara: Princess of Princesses, India, 1627 (The Royal Diaries)*.
- ☐ Lasky, Kathryn. *Kazunomiya: Prisoner of Heaven, Japan, 1858 (The Royal Diaries)*.
- ☐ Lasky, Katherine. *Marie Antoinette: Princess of Versailles, Austria-France, 1769 (The Royal Diaries)*.
- ☐ McKissack, Patricia. *Nzingha: Warrior Queen of Matamba, Angola, Africa, 1595 (The Royal Diaries)*.
- ☐ Meyer, Carolyn. *Kristina: The Girl King, Sweden, 1638 (The Royal Diaries)*.

Horrible Histories

- ☐ Deary, Terry. *Vile Victorians (Horrible Histories)*.
- ☐ Deary, Terry. *Villainous Victorians (Horrible Histories)*.

Modern History (4th-8th Grades)

see also United States History

General Modern History Books (4th-8th Grades)

Taiping Rebellion

- ☐ Patterson, Katherine. *Rebels of the Heavenly Kingdom*.

The American Civil War

- ☐ Denenberg, Barry. *Dear America: When Will This Cruel War Be Over? Gordonsville, Virginia, 1864.*.
- ☐ Hesse, Karen. *Dear America: A Light in the Storm: The Civil War Diary of Amelia Martin, Fenwick Island, Delaware, 1861.*
- ☐ Hite, Sid. *My Name is America: The Journal of Rufus Rowe: A Witness to the Battle of Fredricksburg, Bowling Green, Virginia, 1862.*
- ☐ McKissack, Patricia C. *Dear America: A Picture of Freedom: The Diary of Clotee, a Slave Girl, Belmont Plantation, Virginia, 1859.*

- ☐ Murphy, Jim. *My Name is America: The Journal of James Edmond Pease: A Civil War Union Soldier, Virginia, 1863.*
- ☐ Ratliff, Thomas. *You Wouldn't Want to Be a Civil War Soldier!: A War You'd Rather Not Fight.* ISBN 0531245039
- ☐ Senior, Kathryn. *You Wouldn't Want to Be a Nurse During the American Civil War!: A Job That's Not for the Squeamish.* ISBN 978-0531137864

The Second Reich

- ☐ Heuston, Kimberley. *Otto Von Bismark: Iron Chancellor of Germany (Wicked History).*

Irish Potato Famine

- ☐ Fitzpatrick, Marie-Louise. *The Long March: The Choctaw's Gift to Irish Famine Relief.*
- ☐ Pipe, Jim. *You Wouldn't Want to Sail on an Irish Famine Ship!: A Trip Across the Atlantic You'd Rather not Make.*

The Boxer Rebellion

- ☐ Hood, Ann. *Pearl Buck #3: Jewel of the East (The Treasure Chest).*

World War I

- ☐ Hesse, Karen. *Letters from Rifka.*
- ☐ Levine, Beth Seidel. *Dear America: When Christmas Comes Again: The World War I Diary of Simone Spencer, New York City to the Western Front, 1917.*
- ☐ Whelan, Gloria. *Angel on the Square.*

Russian Revolution

- ☐ Meyer, Carolyn. *Anastasia: The Last Grand Duchess, Russia, 1914 (The Royal Diaries).*

World War II

- [ ] Lasky, Kathryn. Ashes.
- [ ] Auerbacher, Inge. *I Am a Star: Child of the Holocaust.*
- [ ] Bishop, Claire Huchet. *Twenty and Ten.*
- [ ] Borden, Louise. *The Greatest Skating Race: A World War II Story from the Netherlands.*
- [ ] Borden, Louise. *The Journey that Saved Curious George: The True Wartime Escape of Margret and H.A. Rey*
- [ ] Borden, Louise. *The Little Ships: The Heroic Rescue at Dunkirk in World War II.*
- [ ] DeJong, Meindert. *The House of Sixty Fathers.*
- [ ] Foreman, Michael. *War Game: Village Green to No-Man's-Land.*
- [ ] Lowry, Lois. *Number the Stars.*
- [ ] Otsuka, Julie. *When the Emperor was Divine.* World War II, Japanese Internment.
- [ ] Tunnell, Michael O. *Candy Bomber: The Story of the Berlin Airlift's "Chocolate Pilot."*
- [ ] Seredy, Kate. *The Singing Tree.*
- [ ] Sheinkin, Steve. *Bomb: The Race to Build--and Steal--the World's Most Dangerous Weapon.*
- [ ] Tak, Bibi Dumon. *Soldier Bear.* World War II, Poland
- [ ] Warren, Andrea. *Surviving Hitler: A Boy in the Nazi Death Camps.*
- [ ] *Wilbur, Helen.* Lily's Victory Garden.
- [ ] Wood, Douglas. Franklin and Winston: A Christmas that Changed the World.
- [ ] Yolen, Jan. *The Devil's Arithmatic.*

North Korea/Japanese Occupation

- [ ] Choi, Sook Nyul. *Year of Impossible Goodbyes.*
- [ ] Park, Linda Sue. *When My Name was Keoko.*
- [ ] Watkins, Yoko Kawashima. *So Far from the Bamboo Grove.*

Russia under Stalin/Cold War

- [ ] Hautzig, Esther. *The Endless Steppe: Growing Up in Siberia.*
- [ ] Sis, Peter. *The Wall: Growing Up Behind the Iron Curtain.*
- [ ] Yelchin, Eugene. *Breaking Stalin's Nose.*

Chinese Cultural Revolution

- ☐ Chen, Da. *China's Son: Growing Up in the Cultural Revolution.*
- ☐ Jiang, Ji-li. *Red Scarf Girl: A Memoir of the Cultural Revolution.*
- ☐ Li, Moying. *SnowFalling in Spring: Coming of Age in China During the Cultural Revolution.*
- ☐ Yue, Guo. *Little Leap Forward: A Boy in Beijing.*

Cuban Revolution

- ☐ Flores-Galbis, Enrique. *90 Miles to Havana.*
- ☐ Gonzalez, Christina. *The Red Umbrella.*

The Space Race

- ☐ Ottaviani, Jim. *T-Minus: The Race to the Moon.*
- ☐ Thimmesh, Catherine. *Team Moon: How 400,000 People Landed Apollo 11 on the Moon.*

Vietnam War

- ☐ Lai, Thanhha. *Inside Out and Back Again.* Vietnam War
- ☐ Myers, Walter Dean. *Patrol: An American Soldier in Vietnam.*
- ☐ Warren, Andrea. *Escape from Saigon: How a Vietnam War Orphan Became an American Boy.*
- ☐ Whelan, Gloria. *Goodbye, Vietnam.*
- ☐ White, Ellen Emerson. *My Name is America: The Journal of Patrick Seamus Flaherty: United States Marine Corps, Khe Sanh, Vietnam, 1968.*
- ☐ Young, Marilyn B. *The Vietnam War: A History in Documents. (HS?)*

Cambodia, Khmer Rouge Regime

- ☐ Ho, Minfong. *The Clay Marble.*
- ☐ McCormick, Patricia. *Never Fall Down.* Cambodian, Khmer Rouge.
- ☐ Smith, Icy. *Half Spoon of Rice: A Survival Story of the Cambodian Genocide.*

Fall of Soviet Communism

☐ Schmemann, Serge. *When the Wall Came Down: The Berlin Wall and the Fall of Soviet Communism.*

War in Afghanistan

☐ Ellis, Deborah. *Kids of Kabul: Living Bravely Through a Never-Ending War.*

☐ Mortenson, Greg. *Three Cups of Tea: One Man's Journey to Change the World . . . One Child at a Time.*

Iraq War

☐ Ellis, Deborah. *Children of War: Voices of Iraqi Refugees.*

Sudan Civil War

☐ Applegate, Katherine. *Home of the Brave.*

☐ Park, Linda Sue. *A Long Walk to Water.*

Miscellaneous

☐ KamKwamba, William. *The Boy Who Harnessed the Wind.*

Series of Modern History Books (4th-8th Grades)

You Wouldn't Want to Be . . .

☐ Graham, Ian. *You Wouldn't Want to Be a World War II Pilot!: Air Battles You Might Not Survive.* ISBN 0531205177

☐ Graham, Ian. *You Wouldn't Want to Be on the First Flying Machine!: A High-Soaring Ride You'd Rather Not Take.* ISBN 978-0531230428

☐ Graham, Ian. *You Wouldn't Want to Climb Mount Everest!: A Deadly Journey to the Top of the World.* ISBN 0531137856

☐ Green, Jen. *You Wouldn't Want to Be a Polar Explorer!: An Expedition You'd Rather Not Go On.* ISBN 0531162079

- [ ] MacDonald, Fiona. *You Wouldn't Want to Be a Suffragist!: A Protest Movement That's Rougher Than You Expected.* ISBN 0531219119

- [ ] Malam, John. *You Wouldn't Want to Be a Skyscraper Builder!: A Hazardous Job You'd Rather Not Take.* ISBN English

- [ ] Malam, John. *You Wouldn't Want to Be a Secret Agent During World War II!: A Perilous Mission Behind Enemy Lines.* ISBN 053113783X

- [ ] Morley, Jacqueline. *You Wouldn't Want to Meet Typhoid Mary!: A Deadly Cook You'd Rather Not Know.* ISBN 0531230414

- [ ] Stewart, David. *You Wouldn't Want to Sail on the Titanic!: One Voyage You'd Rather Not Make.* ISBN 0531162109

The Royal Diaries

- [ ] Meyer, Carolyn. *Anastasia: The Last Grand Duchess, Russia, 1914 (The Royal Diaries).*

- [ ] White, Ellen Emerson. *Kaiulani: The People's Princess, Hawaii, 1889 (The Royal Diaries).*

Horrible Histories

- [ ] Deary, Terry. *Frightful first World War (Horrible Histories).*

- [ ] Deary, Terry. *The Twentieth Century (Horrible Histories).*

- [ ] Deary, Terry. *Woeful Second World War (Horrible Histories).*

United States History (4th-8th Grades)

General United States History Books (4th-8th Grades)

- [ ] Asim, Jabari. *Fifty Cents and a Dream: Young Booker T. Washington.*

- [ ] Brown, Don. *Dolley Madison Saves George Washington.*

- [ ] Bruchac, Joseph. *Trail of Tears.*

- [ ] Bulla, Clyde Robert. *Squanto, Friend of the Pilgrims.*

- [ ] Carbone, Elisa. *Blood on the River: James Town, 1607.*

- [ ] Cleveland, Will. *Yo, Millard Fillmore!*

- [ ] Cleveland, Will. *Yo, Sacramento!*

- [ ] Comelissen, Cornelia. *Soft Rain: A Story of the Cherokee Trail of Tears.*

- [ ] Davidson, Margaret. *I Have a Dream: The Story of Martin Luther King.*

- [ ] Fleischman, Sid. *By the Great Horn Spoon.*

- [ ] Harness, Cheryl. *Amazing Impossible Erie Canal.*

- [ ] Jakes, John. *Susanna of the Alamo: A True Story.*

- [ ] Keller, Laurie. *The Scrambled States of America Talent Show.*

- [ ] Keller, Laurie. *The Scrambled States of America.*

- [ ] Krensky, Stephen. *Davy Crockett: A Life on the Frontier.*

- [ ] Krull, Kathleen. *A Boy Named FDR: How Franklin D. Roosevelt Grew Up to Change America.*

- [ ] Krull, Kathleen. *Louisa May's Battle: How the Civil War Led to Little Women.*

- [ ] Kudlinski, Kathleen. *Rosa Parks (Childhood of Famous Americans).*

- [ ] Limbaugh, Rush. *Rush Revere and the Brave Pilgrims: Time-Travel Adventures with Exceptional Americans.*

- [ ] Limbaugh, Rush. *Rush Revere and the First Patriots: Time-Travel Adventures With Exceptional Americans.*

- [ ] McKissack, Patricia. *Sojourner Truth: Ain't I a Woman?*

- [ ] Moss, Marissa. *Nurse, Soldier, Spy: The Story of Sarah Edmonds, a Civil War Hero.*

- [ ] Pinkney, Andrea Davis. *Sit-In: How Four Friends Stood Up by Sitting Down.*

- [ ] Ryan, Pam Munoz. *Amelia and Eleanor Go for a Ride.*

- [ ] Ryan, Pam Munoz. *When Marian Sang: The True Recital of Marian Anderson.*

- [ ] Schanzer, Rosalyn. *How We Crossed The West: The Adventures Of Lewis And Clark.*

- [ ] Sheinkin, Steve. *Lincoln's Grave Robbers.*

- [ ] Sheinkin, Steve. *Two Miserable Presidents: Everything Your Schoolbooks Didn't Tell You About the Civil War.*

- [ ] Sheinkin, Steve. *Which Way to the Wild West?: Everything Your Schoolbooks Didn't Tell You About Westward Expansion.*

- [ ] Stanley, George E. *Frederick Douglass: Abolitionist Hero (Childhood of Famous Americans).*

- [ ] Sterling, Dorothy. *Freedom Train: The Story of Harriet Tubman.*
- [ ] St. George, Judith. *The Journey of the One and Only Declaration of Independence.*
- [ ] Talbott, Hudson. *United Tweets of America: 50 State Birds Their Stories, Their Glories.*
- [ ] Woodruff, Elvira. *George Washington's Socks (Time Travel Adventures).*
- [ ] Yates, Elizabeth. *Amos Fortune, Free Man.*

Series of United States History Books (4th-8th Grades)

Jean Fritz

- [ ] Fritz, Jean. *And Then What Happened, Paul Revere?*
- [ ] Fritz, Jean. *Bully for You, Teddy Roosevelt!*
- [ ] Fritz, Jean. *Can't You Make Them Behave, King George?*
- [ ] Fritz, Jean. *The Double Life of Pocahontas.*
- [ ] Fritz, Jean. *The Great LIttle Madison.*
- [ ] Fritz, Jean. *Harriet Beecher Stowe and the Beecher Preachers.*
- [ ] Fritz, Jean. *Just a Few Words, Mr. Lincoln.*
- [ ] Fritz, Jean. *The Lost Colony of Roanoke.*
- [ ] Fritz, Jean. *Shh! We're Writing the Constitution.*
- [ ] Fritz, Jean. *What's The Big Idea, Ben Franklin?*
- [ ] Fritz, Jean. *Where Do You Think You're Going, Christopher Columbus?*
- [ ] Fritz, Jean. *Where Was Patrick Henry on the 29th of May?*
- [ ] Fritz, Jean. *Who's Saying What in Jamestown, Thomas Savage?*
- [ ] Fritz, Jean. *Who's That Stepping on Plymouth Rock?*
- [ ] Fritz, Jean. *Why Don't You Get a Horse, Sam Adams?*
- [ ] Fritz, Jean. *Will You Sign Here, John Hancock?*
- [ ] Fritz, Jean. *You Want Women to Vote, Lizzie Stanton?*

You Wouldn't Want to Be . . .

☐ Cook, Peter. *You Wouldn't Want to Be at the Boston Tea Party!: Wharf Water Tea You'd Rather Not Drink.*

☐ Cook, Peter. *You Wouldn't Want to Sail on a 19th-Century Whaling Ship!: Grisly Tasks You'd Rather Not Do.* ISBN 978-0531163993

☐ Cook, Peter. *You Wouldn't Want to Sail on the Mayflower!: A Trip That Took Entirely Too Long.* ISBN 053112391X

☐ Graham, Ian. *You Wouldn't Want to Be a World War II Pilot!: Air Battles You Might Not Survive.* ISBN 978-0531205174

☐ Graham, Ian. *You Wouldn't Want to Be in the First Submarine!: An Undersea Expedition You'd Rather Avoid.* ISBN 978-0531219126

☐ Graham, Ian. *You Wouldn't Want to Be on Apollo 13!: A Mission You'd Rather Not Go On.* ISBN 978-0531166505

☐ Graham, Ian. *You Wouldn't Want to Be on the First Flying Machine!: A High-Soaring Ride You'd Rather Not Take.* ISBN 978-0531230428

☐ Graham, Ian. *You Wouldn't Want to Be on the Hindenburg!: A Transatlantic Trip You'd Rather Skip.* ISBN 978-0531210499

☐ Graham, Ian. *You Wouldn't Want to Work on the Hoover Dam!.* ISBN 978-0531209462

☐ Graham, Ian. *You Wouldn't Want to Work on the Railroad!: A Track You'd Rather Not Go Down.* ISBN 978-0531162088

☐ Hicks, Peter. *You Wouldn't Want to Live in a Wild West Town!: Dust You'd Rather Not Settle.* ISBN 978-0531163672

☐ MacDonald, Fiona. *You Wouldn't Want to Sail With Christopher Columbus!: Uncharted Waters You'd Rather Not Cross.* ISBN 978-0531160602

☐ Malam, John. *You Wouldn't Want to Be a Secret Agent During World War II!: A Perilous Mission Behind Enemy Lines.*

☐ Malam, John. *You Wouldn't Want to Be a Skyscraper Builder!: A Hazardous Job You'd Rather Not Take.* ISBN 978-0531210482

☐ Malam, John. *You Wouldn't Want to Be a Worker on the Statue of Liberty!: A Monument You'd Rather Not Build.* ISBN 978-0531219102

☐ Matthews, Rupert. *You Wouldn't Want to Be a Chicago Gangster!: Some Dangerous Characters You'd Better Avoid.* ISBN 0531228258

☐ Morley, Jacqueline. *You Wouldn't Want to Be an American Colonist!: A Settlement You'd Rather Not Start.* ISBN 978-0531245026

☐ Morley, Jacqueline. *You Wouldn't Want to Be an American Pioneer!: A Wilderness You'd Rather Not Tame.* ISBN 053128025X

☐ MacDonald, Fiona. *You Wouldn't Want to Be a Suffragist!: A Protest Movement That's Rougher Than You Expected.* ISBN 978-0531219119

☐ Morley, Jacqueline. *You Wouldn't Want to Explore With Lewis and Clark: An Epic Journey You'd Rather Not Make.* ISBN 978-0531230398

☐ Pipe, Jim. *You Wouldn't Want to Be a Salem Witch!: Bizarre Accusations You'd Rather Not Face.* ISBN 0531210472

☐ Ratliff, Thomas. *You Wouldn't Want to Be a Civil War Soldier!: A War You'd Rather Not Fight.* ISBN 0531245039

☐ Ratliff, Thomas. *You Wouldn't Want to Be a Pony Express Rider!: A Dusty, Thankless Job You'd Rather Not Do.* ISBN 978-0531209479

☐ Ratliff, Thomas. *You Wouldn't Want to Work on the Brooklyn Bridge!: An Enormous Project That Seemed Impossible.* ISBN 978-0531205198

☐ Senior, Kathryn. *You Wouldn't Want to Be a Nurse During the American Civil War!: A Job That's Not for the Squeamish.* ISBN 978-0531137864

☐ Stewart, David. *You Wouldn't Want to Sail on the Titanic!: One Voyage You'd Rather Not Make.* ISBN 978-0531162101

Dear America/My Name is America (arranged chronologically)

☐ Lasky, Kathryn. *A Journey to the New World: The Diary of Remember Patience Whipple, Mayflower, 1620.*

☐ Rinaldi, Ann. *My Name is America: The Journal of Jasper Jonathan Pierce: A Pilgrim boy, Plymouth, 1620.*

☐ Fraustino, Lisa Rowe. *Dear America: I Walk in Dread, The Diary of Deliverance Trembly, Witness to the Salem Witch Trials, Massachusetts Bay Colony, 1691.*

☐ McKissack, Fred. *Dear America: Look to the Hills: The Diary of Lozette Moreau, a French Slave Girl, New York Colony, 1763.*

☐ Osborne, Mary Pope. *Dear America: Standing in the Light: The Captive Diary of Catharine Carey Logan, Delaware Valley, Pennsylvania, 1763.*

☐ Turner, Ann. *Dear America: Love Thy Neighbor: The Tory Diary of Prudence Emerson, Green Marsh, Massachusetts, 1774.*

☐ Denenberg, Barry. *My Name is America: The Journal of William Thomas Emerson: A Revolutionary War Patriot, Boston, Massachusetts, 1774.*

☐ Gregory, Kristiana. *The Winter of Red Snow: The Revolutionary War Diary of Abigail Jane Stewart, Valley Forge, Pennsylvania, 1777.*

☐ Gregory, Kristiana. *Dear America: Cannons at Dawn: The Second Diary of Abigail Jane Stewart, Valley Forge, Pennsylvania, 1779.*

☐ Lasky, Kathryn. *My Name is America: The Journal of Augustus Pelletier: Lewis and Clark Expedition, 1804.*

☐ Garland, Sherry. *Dear America: A Line in the Sand: The Alamo diary of Lucinda Lawrence, Gonzales, Texas, 1836.*

☐ Bruchac, Joseph. *My Name is America: The Journal of Jesse Smoke: A Cherokee Boy, The Trail of Tears, 1838.*

☐ Levine, Ellen. *My Name is America: The Journal of Jedediah Barstow: An Emigrant on the Oregon Trail, Overland, 1845.*

☐ Garland, Sherry. *Dear America: Valley of the Moon: The Diary Of Maria Rosalia de Milagros, Sonoma Valley, Alta California, 1846.*

☐ Philbrick, Rodman. *My Name is America: The Journal of Douglas Allen Deeds: The Donner Party Expedition, 1846.*

☐ Gregory, Kristiana. *Dear America: Across the Wide and Lonesome Prairie: The Diary of Hattie Campbell, The Oregon Trail, 1847.*

☐ Denenberg, Barry. *Dear America: So Far from Home: The Diary of Mary Driscoll, an Irish Mill Girl, Lowell, Massachusetts, 1847.*

☐ McDonald, Megan. *Dear America: All the Stars in the Sky: The Santa Fe Trail Diary of Florrie Mack Ryder, The Santa Fe Trail, 1848.*

☐ Gregory, Kristiana. *Dear America: Seeds of Hope: The Gold Rush Diary of Susanna Fairchild, California Territory, 1849.*

☐ Yep, Laurence. *My Name is America: The Journal of Wong Ming-Chung: A Chinese Miner, California, 1852.*

☐ McKissack, Patricia C. *Dear America: A Picture of Freedom: The Diary of Clotee, a Slave Girl, Belmont Plantation, Virginia, 1859.*

☐ Hesse, Karen. *Dear America: A Light in the Storm: The Civil War Diary of Amelia Martin, Fenwick Island, Delaware, 1861.*

☐ Hite, Sid. *My Name is America: The Journal of Rufus Rowe: A Witness to the Battle of Fredricksburg, Bowling Green, Virginia, 1862.*

☐ Murphy, Jim. *My Name is America: The Journal of James Edmond Pease: A Civil War Union Soldier, Virginia, 1863.*

☐ Denenberg, Barry. *Dear America: When Will This Cruel War Be Over? Gordonsville, Virginia, 1864.*

☐ Turner, Ann. *Dear America: The Girl Who Chased Away Sorrow: The Diary of Sarah Nita, a Navajo Girl, New Mexico, 1864.*

☐ Hansen, Joyce. *Dear America: I Thought My Soul Would Rise and Fly: The Diary of Patsy, a Freed Girl, Mars Bluff, South Carolina, 1865.*

☐ Durbin, William. *My Name is America: The Journal of Sean Sullivan: A Transcontinental Railroad Worker, Nebraska and Points West, 1867.*

☐ Gregory, Kristiana. *Dear America: The Great Railroad Race: The Diary of Libby West, Utah Territory, 1868.*

☐ Bartoletti, Susan Campbell. *Dear America: Down the Rabbit Hole: The Diary of Pringle Rose, Chicago, Illinois, 1871.*

☐ Myers, Walter Dean. *My Name is America: The Journal of Joshua Loper: A Black Cowboy, The Chisholm Trail, 1871.*

☐ Bauer, Marion Dane. *Dear America: Land of the Buffalo Bones: The Diary of Mary Ann Elizabeth Rodgers, an English Girl in Minnesota, New Yeovil, Minnesota, 1873.*

☐ Murphy, Jim. *My Name is America: The Journal of Brian Doyle: A Greenhorn on an Alaskan Whaling Ship, The Florence, 1874.*

☐ Patron, Susan. *Dear America: Behind the Masks, The Diary of Angeline Reddy, Bodie, California, 1880.*

☐ Rinaldi, Ann. *Dear America: My Heart Is on the Ground: The Diary of Nannie Little Rose, a Sioux Girl, Carlisle Indian School, Pennsylvania, 1880.*

☐ Murphy, Jim. *Dear America: My Face to the Wind: The Diary of Sarah Jane Price, a Prairie Teacher, Broken Bow, Nebraska 1881.*

☐ Murphy, Jim. *Dear America: West to a Land of Plenty: The Diary of Teresa Angelino Viscardi, New York to Idaho Territory, 1883.*

☐ Campbell, Susan. *Dear America: A Coal Miner's Bride: The Diary of Anetka Kaminska, Lattimer, Pennsylvania, 1896.*

☐ Bartoletti, Susan Campbell. *My Name is America: The Journal of Finn Reardon: A Newsie, New York City, 1899.*

☐ Lasky, Kathryn. *Dear America: Dreams in the Golden Country: The Diary of Zipporah Feldman, a Jewish Immigrant Girl, New York City, 1903.*

☐ Durbin, William. *My Name is America: The Journal of Otto Peltonen: A Finnish Immigrant, Hibbing, Minnesota, 1905.*

☐ Blundell, Judy. *Dear America: A City Tossed and Broken: The Diary of Minnie Bonner, San Francisco, California, 1906.*

☐ Hopkinson, Deborah. *Dear America: Hear My Sorrow: The Diary of Angela Denoto, a Shirtwaist Worker, New York City, 1909.*

☐ White, Ellen Emerson. *Dear America: Voyage on the Great Titanic: The Diary of Margaret Ann Brady, RMS Titanic, 1912.*

☐ Lowry, Lois. *Dear America: Like the Willow Tree: The Diary of Lydia Amelia Pierce, Portland, Maine, 1918.*

☐ White, Ellen Emerson. *Dear America: Voyage on the Great Titanic: The Diary of Margaret Ann Brady, RMS Titanic, 1912.*

☐ Lasky, Kathryn. *Dear America: A Time for Courage: The Suffragette Diary of Kathleen Bowen, Washington, D.C., 1917.*

☐ Levine, Beth Seidel. *Dear America: When Christmas Comes Again: The World War I Diary of Simone Spencer, New York City to the Western Front, 1917.*

- [ ] McKissack, Patricia. *Dear America: Color Me Dark: The Diary of Nellie Lee Love, the Great Migration North, Chicago, Illinois, 1919.*
- [ ] Lasky, Kathryn. *Dear America: Christmas After All: The Great Depression Diary of Minnie Swift, Indianapolis, Indiana 1932.*
- [ ] Denenberg, Barry. *Dear America: Mirror, Mirror on the Wall: The Diary of Bess Brennan, Perkins School for the Blind, 1932.*
- [ ] Janke, Katelan. *Dear America: Survival in the Storm: The Dust Bowl Diary of Grace Edwards, Dalhart, Texas 1935.*
- [ ] Durbin, William. *My Name is America: The Journal of C.J. Jackson: A Dust Bowl Migrant, Oklahoma to California, 1935.*
- [ ] Denenberg, Barry. *Dear America: One Eye Laughing, The Other Eye Weeping: The Diary of Julie Weiss, Vienna, Austria to New York, 1938.*
- [ ] Larson, Kirby. *Dear America: The Fences Between Us: The diary of Piper Davis, Seattle, Washington, 1941.*
- [ ] Osborne, Mary Pope. *Dear America: My Secret War: The World War II Diary of Madeline Beck, Long Island, New York, 1941.*
- [ ] Denenberg, Barry. *Dear America: Early Sunday Morning: The Pearl Harbor Diary of Amber Billows, Hawaii, 1941.*
- [ ] Denenberg, Barry. *My Name is America: The Journal of Ben Uchida: Citizen 13559, Mirror Lake Internment Camp, California, 1942.*
- [ ] Myers, Walter Dean. *My Name is America: The Journal of Scott Pendleton Collins: A World War II Soldier, Normandy, France, 1944.*
- [ ] Myers, Walter Dean. *My Name is America: We Were Heroes: The Journal of Scott Pendleton Collins, A World War II Soldier, Normandy, France, 1944.*
- [ ] Myers, Walter Dean. *My Name is America: The Journal of Biddy Owens: The Negro Leagues, Birmingham, Alabama, 1948.*
- [ ] Pinkney, Andrea Davis. *Dear America: With the Might of Angels, Hadley, Virginia, 1954.*
- [ ] White, Ellen Emerson. *My Name is America: The Journal of Patrick Seamus Flaherty: United States Marine Corps, Khe Sanh, Vietnam, 1968.*

☐ White, Ellen Emerson. *Dear America: Where Have All the Flowers Gone? The Diary of Molly MacKenzie Flaherty, Boston, Massachusetts, 1968.*

Getting to Know the US Presidents (arranged chronologically by president)

☐ Venezia, Mike. *George Washington: First President 1789-1797 (Getting to Know the Us Presidents).*

☐ Venezia, Mike. *John Adams: Second President 1797-1801 (Getting to Know the U.S. Presidents).*

☐ Venezia, Mike. *Thomas Jefferson: Third President 1801 - 1809 (Getting to Know the Us Presidents).*

☐ Venezia, Mike. *James Madison: Fourth President 1809-1817 (Getting to Know the U.S. Presidents).*

☐ Venezia, Mike. *James Monroe: Fifth President 1817-1825 (Getting to Know the U.S. Presidents).*

☐ Venezia, Mike. *John Quincy Adams: Sixth President 1825-1829 (Getting to Know the U.S. Presidents).*

☐ Venezia, Mike. *Andrew Jackson: Seventh President, 1829-1837 (Getting to Know the U.S. Presidents).*

☐ Venezia, Mike. *Martin Van Buren: Eighth President, 1937-1841 (Getting to Know the U.S. Presidents).*

☐ Venezia, Mike. *William Henry Harrison: Ninth President 1841 (Getting to Know the U.S. Presidents).*

☐ Venezia, Mike. *John Tyler: Tenth President, 1841-1845 (Getting to Know the U.S. Presidents).*

☐ Venezia, Mike. *James K. Polk: Eleventh President, 1845-1849 (Getting to Know the U.S. Presidents).*

☐ Venezia, Mike. *Zachary Taylor: Twelfth President 1849-1850 (Getting to Know the U.S. Presidents).*

☐ Venezia, Mike. *Millard Fillmore: Thirteenth President 1850-1853 (Getting to Know the U.S. Presidents).*

☐ Venezia, Mike. *Franklin Pierce: Fourteenth President 1853-1857 (Getting to Know the U.S. Presidents)*.

☐ Venezia, Mike. *James Buchanan: Fifteenth President 1857-1861 (Getting to Know the U.S. Presidents)*.

☐ Venezia, Mike. *Abraham Lincoln: Sixteenth President 1861-1865 (Getting to Know the Us Presidents)*.

☐ Venezia, Mike. *Andrew Johnson: Seventeenth President 1865-1869 (Getting to Know the U.S. Presidents)*.

☐ Venezia, Mike. *Ulysses S. Grant: Eighteenth President 1869-1877 (Getting to Know the U.S. Presidents)*.

☐ Venezia, Mike. *Rutherford B. Hayes: Nineteenth President 1877-1881 (Getting to Know the U.S. Presidents)*.

☐ Venezia, Mike. *James A. Garfield: Twentieth President 1881 (Getting to Know the U.S. Presidents)*.

☐ Venezia, Mike. *Chester A. Arthur: Twenty-First President 1881-1885 (Getting to Know the U.S. Presidents)*.

☐ Venezia, Mike. *Grover Cleveland: Twenty-Second and Twenty-Fourth President, 1885-1889, 1893-1897 (Getting to Know the U.S. Presidents)*.

☐ Venezia, Mike. *Benjamin Harrison: Twenty-Third President 1889-1893 (Getting to Know the U.S. Presidents)*.

☐ Venezia, Mike. *Grover Cleveland: Twenty-Second and Twenty-Fourth President, 1885-1889, 1893-1897 (Getting to Know the U.S. Presidents)*.

☐ Venezia, Mike. *William McKinley: Twenty-Fifth President 1897-1901 (Getting to Know the U.S. Presidents)*.

☐ Venezia, Mike. *Theodore Roosevelt: Twenty-Sixth President: 1901-1909 (Getting to Know the U.S. Presidents)*.

☐ Venezia, Mike. *William Howard Taft: Twenty-Seventh President (Getting to Know the U.S. Presidents)*.

☐ Venezia, Mike. *Woodrow Wilson: Twenty-Eighth President (Getting to Know the U.S. Presidents)*.

☐ Venezia, Mike. *Warren G. Harding: Twenty-Ninth President (Getting to Know the U.S. Presidents).*

☐ Venezia, Mike. *Calvin Coolidge: Thirtieth President (Getting to Know the U.S. Presidents).*

☐ Venezia, Mike. *Herbert Hoover: Thirty-First President: 1929-1933 (Getting to Know the U.S. Presidents).*

☐ Venezia, Mike. *Franklin D. Roosevelt: Thirty-Second President 1933-1945 (Getting to Know the Us Presidents).*

☐ Venezia, Mike. *Harry S. Truman: Thirty-third President 1945-1953 (Getting to Know the Us Presidents).*

☐ Venezia, Mike. *Dwight D. Eisenhower: Thirty-Fourth President 1953-1961 (Getting to Know the U.S. Presidents).*

☐ Venezia, Mike. *John F. Kennedy: Thirty-Fifth President 1961-1963 (Getting to Know the U.S. Presidents).*

☐ Venezia, Mike. *Lyndon B. Johnson: Thirty-Sixth President 1963-1969 (Getting to Know the U.S. Presidents).*

☐ Venezia, Mike. *Richard M. Nixon: Thirty-Seventh President 1969-1974 (Getting to Know the U.S. Presidents).*

☐ Venezia, Mike. *Gerald R. Ford: Thirty-Eighth President 1974-1977 (Getting to Know the U.S. Presidents).*

☐ Venezia, Mike. *Jimmy Carter: Thirty-Ninth President 1977-1981 (Getting to Know the U.S. Presidents).*

☐ Venezia, Mike. *Ronald Reagan: Fortieth President 1981-1989 (Getting to Know the U.S. Presidents).*

☐ Venezia, Mike. *George Bush: Forty-First President 1989-1993 (Getting to Know the U.S. Presidents).*

☐ Venezia, Mike. *Bill Clinton: Forty-Second President 1993-2001 (Getting to Know the U.S. Presidents)*

☐ Venezia, Mike. *George W. Bush: Forty-Third President 2001-Present (Getting to Know the U.S. Presidents).*

Ann Rinaldi's Great Episodes

- [ ] Rinaldi, Ann. *An Acquaintance with Darkness (Great Episodes)*.
- [ ] Rinaldi, Ann. *A Break with Charity: A Story about the Salem Witch Trials (Great Episodes)*.
- [ ] Rinaldi, Ann. *Cast Two Shadows: The American Revolution in the South (Great Episodes)*.
- [ ] Rinaldi, Ann. *The Coffin Quilt: The Feud Between the Hatfields and the McCoys (Great Episodes)*.
- [ ] Rinaldi, Ann. *Come Juneteenth (Great Episodes)*.
- [ ] Rinaldi, Ann. *Hang a Thousand Trees with Ribbons: The Story of Phillis Wheatley (Great Episodes)*.
- [ ] Rinaldi, Ann. *The Fifth of March: A Story of the Boston Massacre (Great Episodes)*.
- [ ] Rinaldi, Ann. *Finishing Becca: A Story about Peggy Shippen and Benedict Arnold (Great Episodes)*.
- [ ] Rinaldi, Ann. *Juliet's Moon (Great Episodes)*.
- [ ] Rinaldi, Ann. *Keep Smiling Through*.
- [ ] Rinaldi, Ann. *The Last Full Measure*.
- [ ] Rinaldi, Ann. *Leigh Ann's Civil War (Great Episodes)*.
- [ ] Rinaldi, Ann. *The Letter Writer (Great Episodes)*.
- [ ] Rinaldi, Ann. *My Vicksburg*.
- [ ] Rinaldi, Ann. *Numbering the Bones*.
- [ ] Rinaldi, Ann. *Or Give Me Death: A Novel of Patrick Henry's Family (Great Episodes)*.
- [ ] Rinaldi, Ann. *A Ride into Morning: The Story of Tempe Wick (Great Episodes)*.
- [ ] Rinaldi, Ann. *The Secret of Sarah Revere (Great Episodes)*.
- [ ] Rinaldi, Ann. *The Staircase (Great Episodes)*.
- [ ] Rinaldi, Ann. *Taking Liberty: The Story of Oney Judge, George Washington's Runaway Slave*.
- [ ] Rinaldi, Ann. *Time Enough for Drums*.

☐ Rinaldi, Ann. *An Unlikely Friendship: A Novel of Mary Todd LIncoln and Elizabeth Keckley.*

Real Geography Books

Geography Books for K-3rd Grades

World Geography Books (K-3rd Grades)

General World Geography Books (K-3rd Grades)

- ☐ Axworthy, Anni. *Anni's India Diary.*
- ☐ Falconer, Ian. *Olivia Goes to Venice.*
- ☐ Krebs, Laurie. *Off We Go To Mexico.*
- ☐ Krebs, Laurie. *Up and Down the Andes.*
- ☐ Krebs, Laurie. *We All Went on Safari.*
- ☐ Krebs, Laurie. *We're Roaming in the Rainforest.*
- ☐ Krebs, Laurie. *We're Sailing to Galapagos.*
- ☐ Krebs, Laurie. *We're Sailing Down the Nile.*
- ☐ Langen, Annette. *Felix and the Flying Suitcase Adventure.* Abbeville Press, 1997.
- ☐ Langen, Annette. *Felix Explores Planet Earth.* Abbeville Press, 1997.
- ☐ Langen, Annette. *Felix Joins the Circus.* Abbeville Press, 2000. Leedy, Loreen. *Blast Off to Earth!: A Look at Geography.* Holiday House, 1992.
- ☐ Langen, Annette. *Felix's Christmas Around the World.* Parklane Publishing, 2003.
- ☐ Langen, Annette. *Felix Travels Back in Time.* Abbeville Press, 1995.
- ☐ Langen, Annette. *Letters from Felix: A Little Rabbit on a World Tour.* Parklane Publishing, 2003.
- ☐ Leedy, Loreen. *Mapping Penny's World.* Square Fish, 2003.
- ☐ Lewin, Ted: *Lost City: The Discovery of Machu Picchu.*
- ☐ Lewin, Ted. *Sacred River: The Ganges of India.*
- ☐ Lewis, J. Patrick. *A World of Wonders: Geographic Travels in Verse and Rhyme.* HarperCollins, 2004.
- ☐ Nobleman, Marc Tyler. *The Felix Activity Book: For Young Globe-Trotter and Time Traveler.* Abbeville Press, 1996.

- [ ] Petty, Kate. *The Amazing Pop-Up Geography Book (Amazing Pop-Ups).* Dutton Juvenile, 2000.
- [ ] Priceman, Margorie. *How to Make a Cherry Pie and See the USA. ISBN-13: 978-0375812552*
- [ ] Priceman, Margorie. *How to Make an apple Pie and See the World. ISBN-10: 0679880836*
- [ ] Rabe, Tish. *There's a Map on My Lap.* Random House Books for Young Readers, 2002.
- [ ] Schuett, Stacey. *Somewhere in the World Right Now. ISBN-13: 978-0679885498*
- [ ] Smith, David. *If the World Were a Village.* Kids Can Press, 2002.
- [ ] Thompson, Kay. *Eloise in Paris.*
- [ ] Thompson, Kay. *Eloise in Moscow.*

General World Geography Books (K-3rd Grades)

Discover the World Alphabet Books

- [ ] Bajaj, Varsha. *T is for Taj Mahal: An India Alphabet Book (Discover the World).* ISBN 1585365041
- [ ] Crane, Carol. *D is for Dancing Dragon: A China Alphabet (Discover the World).* Sleeping Bear Press, 2009.
- [ ] Edwards, Pamela Duncan. *B Is for Big Ben: An England Alphabet (Discover the World).* ISBN 1585363057
- [ ] Grodin, Elissa. *C isfor Ciao: An Italy Alphabet (Discover the World).* ISBN 1585363618
- [ ] Scillian, Devin. *P is for Passport: A World Alphabet (Discover the World).* Sleeping Bear Press, 2003.
- [ ] Wargin, Kathy-jo. *D is for Dala horse: A Nordic Countries Alphabet (Discover the World).* ISBN 1585365106
- [ ] Whelan, Gloria. *K is for Kabuki: A Japan Alphabet (Discover the World).* Sleeping Bear Press, 2009.

☐ Wilbur, Helen. *E is for Eiffel Tower: A France Alphabet (Discover the World).* ISBN 158536505X

United States Geography Books (K-3rd Grades)

General United States Geography Books (K-3rd Grades)

☐ Keller, Laurie. *The Scrambled States of America.* Square Fish, 2002.

☐ Keller, Laurie. *The Scrambled States of America Talent Show.* Henry Holt and Co., 2008.

☐ Scillian, Devin. *A is for America.* Sleeping Bear Press, 2001.

Series of United States Geography Books (K-3rd Grades)

Larry Get Lost

☐ Mullin, Michael. *Larry Gets Lost in Alaska.*

☐ Mullin, Michael. *Larry Gets Lost in Boston.*

☐ Mullin, Michael. *Larry Gets Lost in Chicago.*

☐ Mullin, Michael. *Larry Gets Lost in Los Angeles.*

☐ Mullin, Michael. *Larry Gets Lost in New York City.*

☐ Mullin, Michael. *Larry Gets Lost in Philadelphia.*

☐ Mullin, Michael. *Larry Gets Lost in Portland.*

☐ Mullin, Michael. *Larry Gets Lost in San Francisco.*

☐ Mullin, Michael. *Larry Gets Lost in Texas.*

☐ Mullin, Michael. *Larry Gets Lost in the Twin Cities.*

☐ Mullin, Michael. *Larry Gets Lost in Seattle.*

Discover America State by State (arranged alphabetically by state)

☐ Crane, Carol. *Y is for Yellowhammer: An Alabama Alphabet (Discover America State by State).* Sleeping Bear Press, 2003.

☐ Crane, Carol. *L is for Last Frontier: An Alaska Alphabet (Discover America State by State).* Sleeping Bear Press, 2002.

☐ Gowan, Barbara. *G is for Grand Canyon: An Arizona Alphabet (Discover America State by State)*. Sleeping Bear Press, 2002.

☐ Shoulders, Michael. *N is for Natural State: An Arkansas Alphabet (Discover America State by State)*. Sleeping Bear Press, 2011.

☐ Domeniconi, David. *G is for Golden: A California Alphabet (Discover America State by State)*. Sleeping Bear Press, 2002.

☐ Whitney, Louise. *C is for Centennial: A Colorado Alphabet (Discover America State by State)*. Sleeping Bear Press, 2002.

☐ Grodin, Elissa. *N is for Nutmeg: A Connecticut Alphabet (Discover America State by State)*. Sleeping Bear Press, 2003.

☐ Crane, Carol. *F is for First State: A Delaware Alphabet (Discover America State by State)*. Sleeping Bear Press, 2005.

☐ Crane, Carol. *S Is For Sunshine: A Florida Alphabet. (Discover America State By State. Alphabet Series)*. Sleeping Bear Press, 2000.

☐ Crane, Carol. *P is for Peach: A Georgia Alphabet (Discover America State by State)*. Sleeping Bear Press, 2010.

☐ Goldsberry, U'iliani. *A is for Aloha: A Hawai'i Alphabet (Discover America State by State)*. Sleeping Bear Press, 2010.

☐ Steiner, Stan. *P is for Potato: An Idaho Alphabet (Discover America State by State)*. Sleeping Bear Press, 2005.

☐ Wargin, Kathy-jo. *L is for Lincoln: An Illinois Alphabet (Discover America State By State. Alphabet Series)*. Sleeping Bear Press, 2000.

☐ Reynolds, Cynthia Furlong. *H is for Hoosier: An Indiana Alphabet (Discover America State by State)*. Sleeping Bear Press, 2010.

☐ Pierce, Patricia. *H is for Hawkeye: An Iowa Alphabet (Discover America State by State)*. Sleeping Bear Press, 2003.

☐ Scillian, Devin. *S is for Sunflower: A Kansas Alphabet (Discover America State by State)*. Sleeping Bear Press, 2004.

☐ Riehle, Mary Ann McCabe. *B is for Bluegrass: A Kentucky Alphabet (Discover America State by State)*. Sleeping Bear Press, 2002.

☐ Prieto, Anita. *P is for Pelican: A Louisiana Alphabet (Discover America State by State)*. Sleeping Bear Press, 2004.

☐ Reynolds, Cynthia Furlong. *L is For Lobster: A Maine Alphabet. (Discover America State By State. Alphabet Series)*. Sleeping Bear Press, 2001.

☐ Menendez, Shirley. *B is for Blue Crab: A Maryland Alphabet (Discover America State by State)*. Sleeping Bear Press, 2004.

☐ Kane, Kristen. *M Is For Mayflower: A Massachusetts Alphabet (Discover America State by State)*. Sleeping Bear Press, 2003.

☐ Appleford, Annie. *M Is For Mitten: A Michigan Alphabet Edition 1. (Discover America State By State. Alphabet Series)*. Sleeping Bear Press, 1999.

☐ Wargin, Kathy-jo. *V is for Viking: A Minnesota Alphabet (Discover America State by State)*. Sleeping Bear Press, 2003.

☐ Shoulders, Michael. *M is for Magnolia: A Mississippi Alphabet Book (Discover America State by State)*. Sleeping Bear Press, 2003.

☐ Young, Ross B. *S is for Show Me: A Missouri Alphabet (Discover America State by State)*. Sleeping Bear Press, 2001.

☐ Collard, Sneed B. *B is for Big Sky Country: A Montana Alphabet (Discover America State by State)*. Sleeping Bear Press, 2003.

☐ Shepherd, Rajean Luebs. C is for Cornhusker: *A Nebraska Alphabet (Discover America State by State)*. Sleeping Bear Press, 2004.

☐ Coerr, Eleanor. *S is for Silver: A Nevada Alphabet (Discover America State by State)*. Sleeping Bear Press, 2004.

☐ Harris, Marie. *G is for Granite: A New Hampshire Alphabet (Discover America State by State)*. Sleeping Bear Press, 2002.

☐ Cameron, Eileen. *G is for Garden State: A New Jersey Alphabet (Discover America State by State)*. Sleeping Bear Press, 2004.

☐ James, Helen Foster. *E is for Enchantment: A New Mexico Alphabet (Discover America State by State)*. Sleeping Bear Press, 2004.

☐ Burg, Ann E. *E is for Empire: A New York Alphabet (Discover America State by State)*. Sleeping Bear Press, 2010.

☐ Crane, Carol. *T is for Tar Heel: A North Carolina Alphabet (Discover America State by State)*. Sleeping Bear Press, 2003.

☐ Salonen, Roxane. *P is for Peace Garden: A North Dakota Alphabet (Discover America State by State)*. Sleeping Bear Press, 2005.

☐ Schonberg, Marcia. *B Is For Buckeye: An Ohio Alphabet Edition 1. (Discover America State By State. Alphabet Series)*. Sleeping Bear Press, 2000.

☐ Scillian, Devin. *S is for Sooner: An Oklahoma Alphabet (Discover America State by State)*. Sleeping Bear Press, 2010.

☐ Smith, Marie. *B is for Beaver: An Oregon Alphabet (Discover America State by State)*. Sleeping Bear Press, 2003.

☐ Kane, Kristen. *K is for Keystone: A Pennsylvania Alphabet (Discover America State by State)*. Sleeping Bear Press, 2003.

☐ Allio, Mark R. *R is for Rhode Island Red: A Rhode Island Alphabet (Discover America State by State)*. Sleeping Bear Press, 2005.

☐ Cane, Carol. *P is for Palmeto: A South Carolina Alphabet (Discover America State by State)*. Sleeping Bear Press, 2010.

☐ Anderson, William. *M is for Mount Rushmore: A South Dakota Alphabet (Discover America State by State)*. Sleeping Bear Press, 2005.

☐ Shoulders, Michael. *V is for Volunteer: A Tennessee Alphabet (Discover America State by State)*. Sleeping Bear Press, 2001.

☐ Stacy, Alan. *L Is for Lone Star: A Texas Alphabet (Alphabet Series)*. Sleeping Bear Press, 2001.

☐ Hall, Becky. *A is for Arches: A Utah Alphabet (Discover America State by State)*. Sleeping Bear Press, 2004.

☐ Reynolds, Cynthia Furlong. *M is for Maple Syrup: A Vermont Alphabet (Discover America State by State)*. Sleeping Bear Press, 2002.

☐ Edwards, Pamela Duncan. *O is for Old Dominion: A Virginia Alphabet (Discover America State By State. Alphabet Series)*. Sleeping Bear Press, 2005.

☐ Smith, Roland. *E is for Evergreen: A Washington State Alphabet (Discover America State by State)*. Sleeping Bear Press, 2004.

- [ ] Riehle, Mary Ann McCabe. *M is for Mountain State: A West Virginia Alphabet (Discover America State by State)*. Sleeping Bear Press, 2004.
- [ ] Wargin, Kathy-jo. *B is for Badger: A Wisconsin Alphabet (Discover America State By State. Alphabet Series)*. Sleeping Bear Press, 2004.
- [ ] Gagliano, Eugene. *C is for Cowboy: A Wyoming Alphabet (Discover America State by State)*. Sleeping Bear Press, 2003.

Geography Puzzles (K-3rd Grades)

- [ ] *GeoPuzzle Africa and the Middle East*. GeoToys.
- [ ] *GeoPuzzle Asia*. GeoToys.
- [ ] *GeoPuzzle Europe*. GeoToys.
- [ ] *GeoPuzzle Latin America*. GeoToys.
- [ ] *GeoPuzzle U.S.A. and Canada*. GeoToys.

Geography Books for 4th-8th Grades

World Geography Books (4th-8th Grades)

General World Geography Books (4th-8th Grades)

- [ ] Bjork, Cristina. *Vendela in Venice*.
- [ ] Brassey, Richard. *The Story of London*.
- [ ] Brassey, Richard. *The Story of Scotland*.
- [ ] Chin, Jason. *Island: A Story of the Galápagos*.
- [ ] Chin, Jason. *Redwoods*.
- [ ] Knight, Joan. *Charlotte in Giverny*.
- [ ] Knight, Joan. *Charlotte in London*.
- [ ] Knight, Joan. *Charlotte in New York*.
- [ ] Knight, Joan. *Charlotte in Paris*.
- [ ] Smith, David J. *If the World Were a Village*.

Series of World Geography Books (4th-8th Grades)

Horrible Geography

- [ ] Ganeri, Anita. *Bloomin' Rainforests (Horrible Geography)*. Scholastic, 2008.
- [ ] Ganeri, Anita. *Cracking Coasts (Horrible Geography)*. Scholastic, 2008.
- [ ] Ganeri, Anita. *Desperate Deserts (Horrible Geography)*. Scholastic, 2008.
- [ ] Ganeri, Anita. *Earth-Shattering Earthquakes (Horrible Geography)*. Scholastic, 2008.
- [ ] Ganeri, Anita. *Freaky Peaks (Horrible Geography)*. Scholastic, 2008.
- [ ] Ganeri, Anita. *Geography of the World (Horrible Geography)*. Scholastic, 2008.
- [ ] Ganeri, Anita. *Monster Lakes (Horrible Geography)*. Scholastic, 2008.
- [ ] Ganeri, Anita. *Odious Oceans (Horrible Geography)*. Scholastic, 2008.
- [ ] Ganeri, Anita. *Perishing Poles (Horrible Geography)*. Scholastic, 2008.
- [ ] Ganeri, Anita. *Raging Rivers (Horrible Geography)*. Scholastic, 2008.
- [ ] Ganeri, Anita. *Stormy Weather (Horrible Geography)*. Scholastic, 2008.
- [ ] Ganeri, Anita. *Violent Volcanoes (Horrible Geography)*. Scholastic, 2008.
- [ ] Ganeri, Anita. *Wild Islands (Horrible Geography)*. Scholastic, 2008.

This is . . .

- [ ] Sasek, Miroslav. *This is Australia.* ISBN 0789318547
- [ ] Sasek, Miroslav. *This is Britain.* ISBN 0789315955
- [ ] Sasek, Miroslav. *This is Edinburgh.* ISBN 0789313871
- [ ] Sasek, Miroslav. *This is Greece.* ISBN 0789318555
- [ ] Sasek, Miroslav. *This is Hong Kong.* ISBN 0789315602
- [ ] Sasek, Miroslav. *This is Ireland.* ISBN 0789312247
- [ ] Sasek, Miroslav. *This is Israel.* ISBN 0789315955
- [ ] Sasek, Miroslav. *This is London.* ISBN 0789310627
- [ ] Sasek, Miroslav. *This is Munich.* ISBN 0789324261
- [ ] Sasek, Miroslav. *This is New York.* ISBN 0789308843
- [ ] Sasek, Miroslav. *This is Paris.* ISBN 0789310635
- [ ] Sasek, Miroslav. *This is Rome.* ISBN 0789315491

- ☐ Sasek, Miroslav. *This is San Francisco.* ISBN 0789309629
- ☐ Sasek, Miroslav. *This is Venice.* ISBN 0789312239

Discover the World Alphabet Books (in alphabetical order by country)

- ☐ Bajaj, Varsha. *T is for Taj Mahal: An India Alphabet Book (Discover the World).* ISBN 1585365041
- ☐ Crane, Carol. *D is for Dancing Dragon: A China Alphabet (Discover the World).* Sleeping Bear Press, 2009.
- ☐ Edwards, Pamela Duncan. *B Is for Big Ben: An England Alphabet (Discover the World).* ISBN 1585363057 Scillian, Devin. *P is for Passport: A World Alphabet (Discover the World).* Sleeping Bear Press, 2003.
- ☐ Grodin, Elissa. *C isfor Ciao: An Italy Alphabet (Discover the World).* ISBN 1585363618
- ☐ Wargin, Kathy-jo. *D is for Dala horse: A Nordic Countries Alphabet (Discover the World).* ISBN 1585365106
- ☐ Whelan, Gloria. *K is for Kabuki: A Japan Alphabet (Discover the World).* Sleeping Bear Press, 2009.
- ☐ Wilbur, Helen. *E is for Eiffel Tower: A France Alphabet (Discover the World).* ISBN 158536505X

United States Geography Books (4th-8th Grades)

General United States Geography Books (4th-8th Grades)

- ☐ Holling, Holling C. *Minn of the Mississippi.* Houghton Mifflin Company, 1978.
- ☐ Holling, Holling C. *Paddle-to-the-Sea.* Sandpiper, 1980.
- ☐ Holling, Holling C. *Seabird.* Sandpiper, 1978.
- ☐ Holling, Holling C. *Tree in the Trail.* Sandpiper, 1990.
- ☐ Keller, Laurie. *The Scrambled States of America.* Square Fish, 2002.
- ☐ Keller, Laurie. *The Scrambled States of America Talent Show.* Henry Holt and Co., 2008.
- ☐ Smith, David. *If America Were a Village.* Kids Can Press, 2009.

Series of United States Geography Books (4th-8th Grades)

Discover America State by State (arranged alphabetically by state)

☐ Crane, Carol. *Y is for Yellowhammer: An Alabama Alphabet (Discover America State by State)*. Sleeping Bear Press, 2003.

☐ Crane, Carol. *L is for Last Frontier: An Alaska Alphabet (Discover America State by State)*. Sleeping Bear Press, 2002.

☐ Gowan, Barbara. *G is for Grand Canyon: An Arizona Alphabet (Discover America State by State)*. Sleeping Bear Press, 2002.

☐ Shoulders, Michael. *N is for Natural State: An Arkansas Alphabet (Discover America State by State)*. Sleeping Bear Press, 2011.

☐ Domeniconi, David. *G is for Golden: A California Alphabet (Discover America State by State)*. Sleeping Bear Press, 2002.

☐ Whitney, Louise. *C is for Centennial: A Colorado Alphabet (Discover America State by State)*. Sleeping Bear Press, 2002.

☐ Grodin, Elissa. *N is for Nutmeg: A Connecticut Alphabet (Discover America State by State)*. Sleeping Bear Press, 2003.

☐ Crane, Carol. *F is for First State: A Delaware Alphabet (Discover America State by State)*. Sleeping Bear Press, 2005.

☐ Crane, Carol. *S Is For Sunshine: A Florida Alphabet. (Discover America State By State. Alphabet Series)*. Sleeping Bear Press, 2000.

☐ Crane, Carol. *P is for Peach: A Georgia Alphabet (Discover America State by State)*. Sleeping Bear Press, 2010.

☐ Goldsberry, U'iliani. *A is for Aloha: A Hawai'i Alphabet (Discover America State by State)*. Sleeping Bear Press, 2010.

☐ Steiner, Stan. *P is for Potato: An Idaho Alphabet (Discover America State by State)*. Sleeping Bear Press, 2005.

☐ Wargin, Kathy-jo. *L is for Lincoln: An Illinois Alphabet (Discover America State By State. Alphabet Series)*. Sleeping Bear Press, 2000.

☐ Reynolds, Cynthia Furlong. *H is for Hoosier: An Indiana Alphabet (Discover America State by State)*. Sleeping Bear Press, 2010.

☐ Pierce, Patricia. *H is for Hawkeye: An Iowa Alphabet (Discover America State by State).* Sleeping Bear Press, 2003.

☐ Scillian, Devin. *S is for Sunflower: A Kansas Alphabet (Discover America State by State).* Sleeping Bear Press, 2004.

☐ Riehle, Mary Ann McCabe. *B is for Bluegrass: A Kentucky Alphabet (Discover America State by State).* Sleeping Bear Press, 2002.

☐ Prieto, Anita. *P is for Pelican: A Louisiana Alphabet (Discover America State by State).* Sleeping Bear Press, 2004.

☐ Reynolds, Cynthia Furlong. *L is For Lobster: A Maine Alphabet. (Discover America State By State. Alphabet Series).* Sleeping Bear Press, 2001.

☐ Menendez, Shirley. *B is for Blue Crab: A Maryland Alphabet (Discover America State by State).* Sleeping Bear Press, 2004.

☐ Kane, Kristen. *M Is For Mayflower: A Massachusetts Alphabet (Discover America State by State).* Sleeping Bear Press, 2003.

☐ Appleford, Annie. *M Is For Mitten: A Michigan Alphabet Edition 1. (Discover America State By State. Alphabet Series).* Sleeping Bear Press, 1999.

☐ Wargin, Kathy-jo. *V is for Viking: A Minnesota Alphabet (Discover America State by State).* Sleeping Bear Press, 2003.

☐ Shoulders, Michael. *M is for Magnolia: A Mississippi Alphabet Book (Discover America State by State).* Sleeping Bear Press, 2003.

☐ Young, Ross B. *S is for Show Me: A Missouri Alphabet (Discover America State by State).* Sleeping Bear Press, 2001.

☐ Collard, Sneed B. *B is for Big Sky Country: A Montana Alphabet (Discover America State by State).* Sleeping Bear Press, 2003.

☐ Shepherd, Rajean Luebs. C is for Cornhusker: *A Nebraska Alphabet (Discover America State by State).* Sleeping Bear Press, 2004.

☐ Coerr, Eleanor. *S is for Silver: A Nevada Alphabet (Discover America State by State).* Sleeping Bear Press, 2004.

☐ Harris, Marie. *G is for Granite: A New Hampshire Alphabet (Discover America State by State).* Sleeping Bear Press, 2002.

☐ Cameron, Eileen. *G is for Garden State: A New Jersey Alphabet (Discover America State by State)*. Sleeping Bear Press, 2004.

☐ James, Helen Foster. *E is for Enchantment: A New Mexico Alphabet (Discover America State by State)*. Sleeping Bear Press, 2004.

☐ Burg, Ann E. *E is for Empire: A New York Alphabet (Discover America State by State)*. Sleeping Bear Press, 2010.

☐ Crane, Carol. *T is for Tar Heel: A North Carolina Alphabet (Discover America State by State)*. Sleeping Bear Press, 2003.

☐ Salonen, Roxane. *P is for Peace Garden: A North Dakota Alphabet (Discover America State by State)*. Sleeping Bear Press, 2005.

☐ Schonberg, Marcia. *B Is For Buckeye: An Ohio Alphabet Edition 1. (Discover America State By State. Alphabet Series)*. Sleeping Bear Press, 2000.

☐ Scillian, Devin. *S is for Sooner: An Oklahoma Alphabet (Discover America State by State)*. Sleeping Bear Press, 2010.

☐ Smith, Marie. *B is for Beaver: An Oregon Alphabet (Discover America State by State)*. Sleeping Bear Press, 2003.

☐ Kane, Kristen. *K is for Keystone: A Pennsylvania Alphabet (Discover America State by State)*. Sleeping Bear Press, 2003.

☐ Allio, Mark R. *R is for Rhode Island Red: A Rhode Island Alphabet (Discover America State by State)*. Sleeping Bear Press, 2005.

☐ Cane, Carol. *P is for Palmeto: A South Carolina Alphabet (Discover America State by State)*. Sleeping Bear Press, 2010.

☐ Anderson, William. *M is for Mount Rushmore: A South Dakota Alphabet (Discover America State by State)*. Sleeping Bear Press, 2005.

☐ Shoulders, Michael. *V is for Volunteer: A Tennessee Alphabet (Discover America State by State)*. Sleeping Bear Press, 2001.

☐ Stacy, Alan. *L Is for Lone Star: A Texas Alphabet (Alphabet Series)*. Sleeping Bear Press, 2001.

☐ Hall, Becky. *A is for Arches: A Utah Alphabet (Discover America State by State)*. Sleeping Bear Press, 2004.

- [ ] Reynolds, Cynthia Furlong. *M is for Maple Syrup: A Vermont Alphabet (Discover America State by State)*. Sleeping Bear Press, 2002.
- [ ] Edwards, Pamela Duncan. *O is for Old Dominion: A Virginia Alphabet (Discover America State By State. Alphabet Series)*. Sleeping Bear Press, 2005.
- [ ] Smith, Roland. *E is for Evergreen: A Washington State Alphabet (Discover America State by State)*. Sleeping Bear Press, 2004.
- [ ] Riehle, Mary Ann McCabe. *M is for Mountain State: A West Virginia Alphabet (Discover America State by State)*. Sleeping Bear Press, 2004.
- [ ] Wargin, Kathy-jo. *B is for Badger: A Wisconsin Alphabet (Discover America State By State. Alphabet Series)*. Sleeping Bear Press, 2004.
- [ ] Gagliano, Eugene. *C is for Cowboy: A Wyoming Alphabet (Discover America State by State)*. Sleeping Bear Press, 2003.

Geography Puzzles (4th-8th Grades)

- [ ] *GeoPuzzle Africa and the Middle East.* GeoToys.
- [ ] *GeoPuzzle Asia.* GeoToys.
- [ ] *GeoPuzzle Europe.* GeoToys.
- [ ] *GeoPuzzle Latin America.* GeoToys.
- [ ] *GeoPuzzle U.S.A. and Canada.* GeoToys.

Geography Games (4th-8th Grades)

- [ ] *10 Days in Africa Game.* Out of the Box, 2008.
- [ ] *10 Days in Asia Game.* Out of the Box, 2008.
- [ ] *10 Days in Europe Game.* Out of the Box, 2008.
- [ ] *10 Days in the USA Game.* Out of the Box, 2008.

Real Literature Books

Literature Books for K-3rd Grades

Ancient Literature (K-3rd Grades)

- [ ] Daily, Don. *The Classic Treasury of Aesop's Fables.* Running Press Kids, 2007.

- [ ] D'Aulaire, Ingri and Edgar. *D'Aulaires' Book of Greek Myths.* Delacorte Books for Young Reader, 1992.

- [ ] Hastings, Selina. *The Children's Illustrated Bible.* DK Children, 2005.

- [ ] Johnson, Spencer. *The Value of Honesty: The Story of Confucius.* Value Communications, 1979.

- [ ] Little, Emily. *The Trojan Horse: How the Greeks Won the War (Step-Into-Reading, Step 5).* Random House Books for Young Readers, 1998.

- [ ] Moore, Christopher. *Ishtar and Tammuz: A Babylonian Myth of the Seasons.* HarperCollins, 1997.

- [ ] Novesky, Amy. *Elephant Prince: The Story of Ganesh.* Mandala Publishing, 2004.

- [ ] Osborne, Mary Pope. *Tales from the Odyssey, Part 1.* Disney/Hyperion Books, 2010.

- [ ] Osborne, Mary Pope. *Tales from the Odyssey, Part 2.* Disney/Hyperion Books, 2010.

- [ ] Rockwell, Anne. *Romulus And Remus (Ready to Read , Level 2).* Simon Spotlight, 1997.

- [ ] Smith, Brendan Powell. *The Brick Bible: A New Spin on the Old Testament.* Skyhorse Publishing, 2011.

- [ ] Smith, Brendan Powell. *The Brick Bible: A New Spin on the Story of Jesus.* Skyhorse Publishing, 2012.

- [ ] Souhami, Jessica. *Rama and the Demon King: An Ancient Tale from India.* Frances Lincoln Children's Books, 2005.

- [ ] Stewart, Whitney. *Becoming Buddha: The Story of Siddhartha.* Heian, 2009.

- ☐ Weiss, Jim. *Egyptian Treasures: Mummies and Myths.* Greathall Productions, 1999.
- ☐ Weiss, Jim. *Greek Myths.* Greathall Productions, 2000.
- ☐ Weiss, Jim. *Heroes in Mythology: Theseus, Prometheus, Odin.* Greathall Productions, 2000.
- ☐ Weiss, Jim. *Jewish Holiday Stories.* Greathall Productions, 2001.
- ☐ Weiss, Jim. *Tales from the Old Testament.* Greathall Productions, 2000.
- ☐ Zeman, Ludmila. *Gilgamesh the King (The Gilgamesh Trilogy 1).* Tundra Books, 1998.
- ☐ Zeman, Ludmila. *The Revenge of Ishtar (The Gilgamesh Trilogy 2).* Tundra Books, 1998.
- ☐ Zeman, Ludmila. *The Last Quest of Gilgamesh (The Gilgamesh Trilogy 3).* Tundra Books, 1998.

Medieval/Renaissance Literature (K-3rd Grades)

- ☐ Ashby, Ruth. *Caedmon's Song.* ISBN 0802852416
- ☐ Chaucer, Geoffrey. *Chanticleer and the Fox.*
- ☐ Chen, Debbie. *Monkey King Wreaks Havoc in Heaven (Adventures of Monkey King).* Pan Asian Publications, 2001.
- ☐ Chen, Debbie. *Tang Monk Disciples Monkey King (Adventures of Monkey King).* Pan Asian Publications, 2005.
- ☐ Hodges, Margaret. *Gulliver in Lilliput.* Holiday House, 1997.
- ☐ Hodges, Margaret. *The Kitchen Knight: A Tale of King Arthur.* ISBN 0823410633
- ☐ Hodges. *Saint George and the Dragon.* Little, Brown Books for Young Readers, 1990.
- ☐ Ingle, Annie. *Robin Hood (A Stepping Stone Book).* Random House Books for Young Readers, 1991.
- ☐ Kimmel, Eric A. *Don Quixote and the Windmills.* Farrar, Straus and Giroux, 2004.
- ☐ Kimmel, Eric A. *The Hero Beowulf.* Farrar, Straus and Giroux, 2005.

☐ Kraus, Robert. *The Making of Monkey King (Adventures of Monkey King, 1).* Pan Asian Publications, 1998.

☐ Strickland, Brad. *Be a Wolf! [Beowulf] (Adventures of Wishbone).* Lyrick Studios, 2004.

☐ Venturini, Claudia. *Ali Baba and the Forty Thieves.* ISBN 1846432510

☐ Weiss, Jim. *Celtic Treasures.* Greathall Productions, 2000. Weiss, Jim. *King Arthur and His Knights.* Greathall Productions, 2000.

☐ Weiss, Jim. *Rip Van Winkle/Gulliver's Travels.* Greathall Productions, 2000.

☐ Weiss, Jim. *Romeo & Juliet.* Greathall Productions, 2005.

☐ Weiss, Jim. *Shakespeare for Children.* Greathall Productions, 2000.

☐ Weiss, Jim. *A Storyteller's Version of... Arabian Nights.* Greathall Productions, 1999.

☐ Weiss, Jim. *Three Musketeers/Robin Hood.* HarperCollins, 1999.

☐ Wisniewski, David. *Sundiata: Lion King of Mali.* Sandpiper, 1999.

☐ Zeman, Ludmila. *Sinbad: From the Tales of the Thousand and One Nights (1).* Tundra Books, 1999.

☐ Zeman, Ludmila. *Sinbad: From the Tales of the Thousand and One Nights (2).* Tundra Books, 2001.

☐ Zeman, Ludmila. *Sinbad's Secret (3).* Tundra Books, 2003.

Early Modern Literature (K-3rd Grades)

☐ Brown, Monica. *My Name Is Gabito/Mi Llamo Gabito: The Life of Gabriel Garcia Marquez/La Vida De Gabriel Garcia Marquez.*

☐ Brown, Monica. *Pablo Neruda: Poet of the People.*

☐ Krull, Kathleen. *The Boy on Fairfield Street: How Ted Geisel Grew Up to Become Dr. Seuss.*

☐ Weiss, Jim. *American Tall Tales.* Greathall Productions, 2003.

☐ Weiss, Jim. *Jungle Book.* Greathall Productions, 2000.

☐ Weiss, Jim. *Mystery! Mystery!.* Greathall Productions, 2000.

☐ Weiss, Jim. *Prince & the Pauper.* Greathall Productions, 2002.

- [ ] Weiss, Jim. *Sherlock Holmes for Children.* Greathall Productions, 2004.
- [ ] Weiss, Jim. *Three Musketeers/Robin Hood.* HarperCollins, 1999.
- [ ] Weiss, Jim. *Treasure Island.* Greathall Productions, 2000.
- [ ] Weiss, Jim. *Twenty Thousand Leagues Under the Sea.* Greathall Productions, 2007.

United States Literature (K-3rd Grades)

- [ ] Adler, David A. *A Picture Book of Frederick Douglass.*
- [ ] Adler, David A. *A Picture Book of Harriet Beecher Stowe.*
- [ ] Avi. *Finding Providence: The Story of Roger Williams.*
- [ ] Bedard, Michael. *Emily.*
- [ ] Brown, Don. *American Boy: The Adventures of Mark Twain.*
- [ ] Catrow, David. *We the Kids: The Preamble to the Constitution.*
- [ ] Cooper, Floyd. *Coming Home: From the LIfe of Langston Hughes.*
- [ ] Crespo, George L. *How the Sea Began.*
- [ ] Goldsmith, Howard. *Mark Twain at Work.*
- [ ] Ita, Sam. *Moby Dick: A Pop-Up Book.*
- [ ] Johnson, D.B. *Henry Builds a Cabin.*
- [ ] Johnson, D.B. *Henry Climbs a Mountain.*
- [ ] Johnson, D.B. *Henry Hikes to Fitchburg.*
- [ ] Johnson, D.B. *Henry Works.*
- [ ] Lewis, Owen Paul. *Frog Girl.*
- [ ] Lewis, Owen Paul. *Storm Boy.*
- [ ] Longfellow, Henry Wadsworth. *Paul Revere's Ride.*
- [ ] Maltbie, Priscilla. *Bambino and Mr. Twain.*
- [ ] McAlpine, Gordon. *The Tell-Tale Start.*
- [ ] McDermott, Gerald. *Arrow to the Sun: A Pueblo Indian Tale.*
- [ ] McDermott, Gerald. *Raven: A Trickster Tale from the Pacific Northwest.*
- [ ] O'Neal, Deborah. *The Trouble with Henry: A Tale of Walden Pond.*
- [ ] Selden, Bernice. *Moby Dick.*

☐ Weiss, Jim. *American Tall Tales.* Greathall Productions, 2003.

☐ Weiss, Jim. *Twenty Thousand Leagues Under the Sea.* Greathall Productions, 2007.

Literature Books for 4th-8th Grades

Ancient Literature (4th-8th Grades)

☐ Bendick, Jeanne. *Herodotus and the Road to History.* Bethlehem Books, 2009.

☐ D'Aulaire, Ingri and Edgar. *D'Aulaires' Book of Greek Myths.* Delacorte Books for Young Reader, 1992.

☐ Demi. *The Legend of Lao Tzu and the Tao Te Ching.* Margaret K. McElderry Books, 2007.

☐ De Zeeuw, P. *Augustine the Farmer's Boy of Tagaste.* Inheritance Pub, 1998.

☐ Green, Roger Lancelyn. *Tales of Ancient Egypt (Puffin Classics).* Puffin, 1996. Henderson, Kathy. *Lugalbanda.* Walker Children's Paperbacks, 2007.

☐ Hastings, Selina. *The Children's Illustrated Bible.* DK Children, 2005.

☐ Jacobs, Joseph. *The Fables of Aesop (Dover Children's Evergreen Classics).* Dover, 2002.

☐ Krishnawsami, Uma. *The Broken Tusk: Stories of the Hindu God Ganesha.* August House, 2006.

☐ Landaw, Jonathan. *Prince Siddhartha: The Story of Buddha.* Wisdom Publication, 2011.

☐ Lively, Penelope. *In Search of a Homeland: The Story of the Aeneid.* Lincoln Children's Books, 2006.

☐ McCaughrean, Geraldine. *Gilgamesh the Hero.* Eerdmans Books for Young Readers, 2003.

☐ Osborne, Mary Pope. *Tales from the Odyssey, Part 1.* Disney/Hyperion Books, 2010.

☐ Osborne, Mary Pope. *Tales from the Odyssey, Part 2.* Disney/Hyperion Books, 2010.

- [ ] Patel, Sanjay. *Ramayana: Divine Loophole.* Chronicle Books, 2010.
- [ ] Smith, Brendan Powell. *The Brick Bible: A New Spin on the Old Testament.* Skyhorse Publishing, 2011.
- [ ] Smith, Brendan Powell. *The Brick Bible: A New Spin on the Story of Jesus.* Skyhorse Publishing, 2012.
- [ ] Sutcliff, Rosemary. *Black Ships Before Troy: The Story of the Iliad.* Laurel Leaf, 2005.

Medieval/Renaissance Literature (4th-8th Grades)

- [ ] Blackwood, Gary. *The Shakespeare Stealer.* Puffin, 2000.
- [ ] Blackwood, Gary. *Shakespeare's Scribe.* Puffin, 2002.
- [ ] Blackwood, Gary. *Shakespeare's Spy.* Puffin, 2005.
- [ ] Burdett, Lois. *Hamlet : For Kids (Shakespeare Can Be Fun series).* Firefly Books, 2000.
- [ ] Burdett, Lois. *MacBeth : For Kids (Shakespeare Can Be Fun series).* Firefly Books, 1996.
- [ ] Burdett, Lois. *A Midsummer Night's Dream : For Kids (Shakespeare Can Be Fun series).* Firefly Books, 1997.
- [ ] Burdett, Lois. *Much Ado About Nothing : For Kids (Shakespeare Can Be Fun series).* Firefly Books, 2002.
- [ ] Burdett, Lois. *Romeo and Juliet : For Kids (Shakespeare Can Be Fun series).* Firefly Books, 1998.
- [ ] Burdett, Lois. *The Tempest : For Kids (Shakespeare Can Be Fun series).* Firefly Books, 1999.
- [ ] Burdett, Lois. *Twelfth Night : For Kids (Shakespeare Can Be Fun series).* Firefly Books, 1994.
- [ ] Burdett, Lois. *A Child's Portrait of Shakespeare : For Kids (Shakespeare Can Be Fun series).* Firefly Books, 1995.
- [ ] Byrd, Robert. *The Hero and the Minotaur.* Dutton Children's Books, 2005.

- [ ] Cervantes, Miguel de. *Don Quixote (Candlewick Illustrated Classic).* HarperCollins, 2004.
- [ ] Chaucer, Geoffrey. *The Canterbury Tales.* Puffin, 1997.
- [ ] D'Aulaire, Ingri. *D'Aulaires' Book of Norse Myths.* New York Review of Books, 2005.
- [ ] Demi. *Marco Polo.* Amazon Children's Publishing, 2008.
- [ ] Demi. *Muhammad.* Margaret K. McElderry Books, 2003.
- [ ] Demi. *Rumi: Persian Poet, Whirling Dervish.* Amazon Children's Publishing, 2009.
- [ ] Jenkins, Martin. *Miguel de Cervantes: Don Quixote.*
- [ ] McCaughrean, Geraldine. *El Cid.* Oxford University Press, 1988.
- [ ] McCaughrean, Geraldine. *One Thousand and One Arabian Nights (Oxford Story Collections).* Oxford University Press, 2000.
- [ ] Montejo, Victor. *Popol Vuh: A Sacred Book of the Maya.* Groundwood Books, 2009.
- [ ] Morpurgo, Michael. *Beowulf.* Candlewick, 2006.
- [ ] Morpurgo, Michael. *Sir Gawain and the Green Knight.* Candlewick, 2004.
- [ ] Moseley, James. *The Ninth Jewel of the Mughal Crown: The Birbal Tales from the Oral Traditions of India.*
- [ ] Strickland, Brad. *Be a Wolf!* [Beowulf] *(Adventures of Wishbone).* Lyrick Studios, 2004.
- [ ] Tusiani, Dante Alighieri Joseph. *Dante's Divine Comedy: As Told for Young People.* Legas, 2001.
- [ ] Wu, Cheng-En. *Adventures of Monkey King.* Victory Press, 1989.

Early Modern Literature (4th-8th Grades)

- [ ] Barkand, Joanne. *A Pup in King Arthur's Court* [A Connecticut Yankee in King Arthur's Court] *(Adventures of Wishbone).* Lyrick Studios, 1998.
- [ ] Barkan, Joanne. *A Tale of Two Sitters* [A Tale of Two Cities] *(Adventures of Wishbone).* Lyrick Studios, 1998.

☐ Butcher, Nancy. *Dr. Jekyll and Mr. Dog* [Dr. Jekyll and Mr. Hyde] *(Adventures of Wishbone)*. Lyrick Studios, 1998.

☐ Crider, Bill. *Muttketeer!* [The Three Musketeers] *(Adventures of Wishbone)*. Lyrick Studios, 1997.

☐ Daly Jude. *The Tale of Paradise Lost: Based on the Poem by John Milton*. HarperCollins, 2004.

☐ Deedy, Carmen Agra. *The Cheshire Cheese Cat: A Dickens of a Tale*. Charles Dickens.

☐ Friedman, Micael Jan. *Hunchdog of Notre Dame* [Hunchback of Notre Dame] *(Adventures of Wishbone)*. Lyrick Studios, 1997.

☐ Friedman, Michael Jan. *The Mutt in the Iron Muzzle* [The Man in the Iron Mask] *(Adventures of Wishbone)*. Lyrick Studios, 1998.

☐ Leavitt, Caroline. *The Prince and the Pooch* [The Prince and the Pauper] *(Adventures of Wishbone #3)*. Lyrick Studios, 1997.

☐ Leavitt, Caroline. *Robinhound Crusoe* [Robinson Crusoe] *(Adventures of Wishbone #4)*. Lyrick Studios, 1997.

☐ Palacios, Argentina. *Adventures of Don Quixote (Dover Children's Thrift Editions)*. Dover Publications, 1999.

☐ Steele, Alexander. *Huckleberry Dog* [Huckleberry Finn] *(Adventures of Wishbone)*. Lyrick Studios, 2000.

☐ Steele, Alexander. *Moby Dog* [Moby Dick] *(Adventures of Wishbone)*. Lyrick Studios, 1998.

☐ Strickland, Brad. *Gullifur's Travels* [Gullliver's Travels] *(Adventures of Wishbone #18)*. Lyrick Studios, 1999.

☐ Strickland, Brad. *Saltly Dog* [Treasure Island] *(Adventures of Wishbone)*. Lyrick Studios, 2004.

☐ Swift, Johnathan. *Jonathan Swift's Gulliver*. Candlewick Press, 2005.

☐ Swift, Johnathan. *Gulliver's Travels (Dover Thrift Editions)*. Dover Publications, 1996.

United States Literature (4th-8th Grades)

☐ Alcott, Louisa May. *Little Women.*

☐ Avi. *Finding Providence: The Story of Roger Williams.*

☐ Baker, Betty. *Walk the World's Rim. [Cabeza de Vaca]*

☐ Burleigh, Robert. *Edna.*

☐ Fink, Sam. *The Declaration Of Independence: The Words That Made America.*

☐ Fink, Sam. *The Gettysburg Address.*

☐ Fritz, Jean. *Harriet Beecher Stowe and the Beecher Preachers.*

☐ Fritz, Jean. *Shh! We're Writing the Constitution.*

☐ Frost, Robert and Jeffers, Susan. *Stopping By Woods on a Snowy Evening.*

☐ Frost, Robert and Young, Ed. *Birches.*

☐ George, Judith St. *The Journey of the One and Only Declaration of Independence.*

☐ Gormley, Beatrice. *Louisa May Alcott (Childhood of Famous Americans).*

☐ Hausman, Gerald. *A Mind with Wings: The Story of Henry David Thoreau.*

☐ Hughes, Lanston. *The Negro Speaks of Rivers.*

☐ Irving, Washington. *Rip Van Winkle & Other Stories.*

☐ Jones, Rebecca C. *Captain John Smith's Big and Beautiful Bay.*

☐ Poe, Edgar Allen. *Edgar Allen Poe's Tales of Mystery and Madness.*

☐ Spires, Elizabeth. *The Mouse of Amherst.*

☐ Stanley, George E. *Frederick Douglass: Abolitionist Hero (Childhood of Famous Americans).*

☐ Twain, Mark. *Adventures of Tom Sawyer.*

☐ Walker, Alice. *Langston Hughes: American Poet.*

☐ Weiss, Jim. *Spooky Classics for Children: The Canterville Ghost / Dr. Heidegger's Experiment / The Sending of Dana Da.*

Real Grammar Books

Grammar Books for K-3rd Grades

General Books on Grammar (K-3rd Grades)

- ☐ Auch, Mary Jane. *The Plot Chickens.* Holiday House, 2010.

- ☐ Barretta, Gene. *Dear Deer: A Book of Homophones.* Square Fish, 2010.

- ☐ Bruno, Elsa Knight. *Punctuation Celebration.* Square Fish, 2012.

- ☐ Carr, Jan. *Greedy Apostrophe: A Cautionary Tale.* Holiday House, 2009.

- ☐ Cleary, Brian P. *The Punctuation Station.* Millbrook Press, 2010.

- ☐ Donohue, Moira Rose. *Alfie the Apostrophe.* Albert Whitman & Company, 2006.

- ☐ Donohue, Moira Rose. *Penny and the Punctuation Bee.* Albert Whitman & Company, 2008.

- ☐ Ferris, Jeri Chase. *Noah Webster and HIs Words,* 2012.

- ☐ Gwynne, Fred. *A Chocolate Moose for Dinner.* Aladdin, 1988.

- ☐ Gwynne, Fred. *The King Who Rained.* Aladdin, 1988.

- ☐ Leedy, Loreen. *Crazy Like a Fox: A Simile Story.* Holiday House, 2009.

- ☐ Leedy, Loreen. *The Furry News: How to Make a Newspaper.* Holiday House, 1990.

- ☐ Leedy, Loreen. *Look at My Book: How Kids Can Write & Illustrate Terrific Books.* Holiday House, 2003.

- ☐ Leedy, Loreen. *Messages in the Mailbox: How to Write a Letter.* Holiday House, 1994.

- ☐ Leedy, Loreen. *There's a Frog in My Throat: 440 Animal Sayings a Little Bird Told Me.* Holiday House, 2003.

- ☐ Lichtenheld, Tom. *E-mergency!.* Chronicle Books, 2011.

- ☐ Maizels Jennie. *The Amazing Pop-up Grammar Book.* Dutton Juvenile, 1996.

- ☐ Petty Kate. *The Perfect Pop-Up Punctuation Book.* Dutton Juvenile, 2006.

- ☐ Pulver, Robin. *Silent Letters Loud and Clear.* Holiday House, 2010.

- [ ] Pulver, Robin. *Nouns and Verbs Have a Field Day.* Holiday House, 2007.
- [ ] Pulver, Robin. *Punctuation Takes a Vacation.* Holiday House, 2004.
- [ ] Pulver, Robin. *Happy Endings: A Story About Suffixes.* Holiday House, 2011.
- [ ] Truss. *Eats, Shoots & Leaves: Why, Commas Really Do Make a Difference!.* Putnam Juvenile, 2006.
- [ ] Truss. *The Girl's Like Spaghetti: Why, You Can't Manage without Apostrophes!.* Putnam Juvenile, 2007.
- [ ] Truss. *Twenty-Odd Ducks: Why, every punctuation mark counts!.* Putnam Juvenile, 2008.
- [ ] Turner, Priscilla. *The War Between the Vowels and the Consonants.* Farrar, Straus and Giroux, 1999.
- [ ] Walker, Sally M. *The Vowel Family: A Tale of Lost Letters.* Carolrhoda Books, 2008.

Series of Grammar Books (K-3rd Grades)

Words are Categorical

- [ ] Cleary, Brian P. *But and For, Yet and Nor: What is a Conjunction? (Words are Categorical).* Carolrhoda, 2012.
- [ ] Cleary, Brian P. *Breezier, Cheesier, Newest, and Bluest: What Are Comparatives and Superlatives? (Words Are Categorical).* Carolrhoda, 2013.
- [ ] Cleary, Brian P. *Cool! Whoa! Ah and Oh!: What Is an Interjection? (Words Are Categorical).* Carolrhoda, 2013.
- [ ] Cleary, Brian P. *Dearly, Nearly, Insincerely: What Is An Adverb? (Words Are Categorical).* Carolrhoda, 2005.
- [ ] Cleary, Brian P. *Feet and Puppies, Thieves and Guppies: What Are Irregular Plurals? (Words Are Categorical).* Carolrhoda, 2012.
- [ ] Cleary, Brian P. *Hairy, Scary, Ordinary: What Is an Adjective? (Words Are Categorical).* Carolrhoda, 2001.
- [ ] Cleary, Brian P. *How Much Can a Bare Bear Bear?: What Are Homonyms and Homophones? (Words Are Categorical).* Carolrhoda, 2007.

☐ Cleary, Brian P. *I And You And Don't Forget Who: What Is a Pronoun? (Words Are Categorical)*. Carolrhoda, 2006.

☐ Cleary, Brian P. *I'm and Won't, They're and Don't: What's a Contraction? (Words Are Categorical)*. Carolrhoda, 2012.

☐ Cleary, Brian P. *Lazily, Crazily, Just a Bit Nasally: More About Adverbs (Words are Categorical)*. Carolrhoda, 2010.

☐ Cleary, Brian P. *A Lime, a Mime, a Pool of Slime: More About Nouns (Words Are Categorical)*. Carolrhoda, 2008.

☐ Cleary, Brian P. *Madam and Nun and 1001: What Is a Palindrome? (Words Are Categorical)*. Carolrhoda, 2012.

☐ Cleary, Brian P. *A Mink, a Fink, a Skating Rink: What Is a Noun? (Words Are Categorical)*. Carolrhoda, 1999.

☐ Cleary, Brian P. *Pitch and Throw, Grasp and Know: What Is a Synonym? (Words Are Categorical)*. Carolrhoda, 2007.

☐ Cleary, Brian P. *Quirky, Jerky, Extra Perky: More About Adjectives (Words Are Categorical)*. Carolrhoda, 2009.

☐ Cleary, Brian P. *Skin Like Milk, Hair of Silk: What Are Similes and Metaphors? (Words Are Categorical)*. Carolrhoda, 2011.

☐ Cleary, Brian P. *Slide and Slurp, Scratch and Burp: More About Verbs (Words Are Categorical)*. Carolrhoda, 2009.

☐ Cleary, Brian P. *Stop and Go, Yes and No: What Is an Antonym? (Words Are Categorical)*. Carolrhoda, 2008.

☐ Cleary, Brian P. *Straight and Curvy, Meek and Nervy: More About Antonyms (Words Are Categorical)*. Carolrhoda, 2011.

☐ Cleary, Brian P. *Stroll and Walk, Babble and Talk: More About Synonyms (Words Are Categorical)*. Carolrhoda, 2010.

☐ Cleary, Brian P. *Thumbtacks, Earwax, Lipstick, Dipstick: What Is a Compound Word? (Words Are Categorical)*. Carolrhoda, 2011.

☐ Cleary, Brian P. *To Root to Toot to Parachute: What Is a Verb (Words Are Categorical)*. Carolrhoda, 2001.

☐ Cleary, Brian P. *Under, Over, by the Clover: What Is a Preposition? (Words Are Categorical)*. Carolrhoda, 2003.

Rick Walton Books

☐ Walton, Rick. *Around the House the Fox Chased the Mouse: Adventures in Prepositions (Language Adventures Book)*. Gibbs Smith, 2011.

☐ Walton, Rick. *Bullfrog Pops!: Adventures in Verbs and Direct Objects (Language Adventures Book)*. Gibbs Smith, 2011.

☐ Walton, Rick. *Herd of Cows, Flock of Sheep: Adventures in Collective Nouns (Language Adventures Book)*. Gibbs Smith, 2011.

☐ Walton, Rick. *Just Me & 6,000 Rats: A Tale of Conjunctions (Language Adventures Book)*. Gibbs Smith, 2011.

☐ Walton, Rick. *Once There Was A Bull...(frog): Adventures in Compound Words (Language Adventures Book)*. Gibbs Smith, 2011.

☐ Walton, Rick. *Pig, Pigger, Piggest: Adventures in Comparing*. Gibbs Smith, 2011.

☐ Walton, Rick. *Suddenly Alligator: Adventures in Adverbs*. Gibbs Smith, 2011.

☐ Walton, Rick. *Why the Banana Split: Adventures in Idioms (Language Adventures Book)*. Gibbs Smith, 2011.

Grammar Books for 4th-8th Grades

General Books on Grammar (4th-8th Grades)

☐ Auch, Mary Jane. *The Plot Chickens*. Holiday House, 2010.

☐ Barretta, Gene. *Dear Deer: A Book of Homophones*. Square Fish, 2010.

☐ Bruno, Elsa Knight. *Punctuation Celebration*. Square Fish, 2012.

☐ Carr, Jan. *Greedy Apostrophe: A Cautionary Tale*. Holiday House, 2009.

☐ Cleary, Brian P. *The Punctuation Station*. Millbrook Press, 2010.

☐ Donohue, Moira Rose. *Alfie the Apostrophe*. Albert Whitman & Company, 2006.

☐ Donohue, Moira Rose. *Penny and the Punctuation Bee*. Albert Whitman & Company, 2008.

☐ Ferris, Jeri Chase. *Noah Webster and HIs Words,* 2012.

☐ Gwynne, Fred. *A Chocolate Moose for Dinner.* Aladdin, 1988.

☐ Gwynne, Fred. *The King Who Rained.* Aladdin, 1988.

☐ Leedy, Loreen. *Crazy Like a Fox: A Simile Story.* Holiday House, 2009.

☐ Leedy, Loreen. *The Furry News: How to Make a Newspaper.* Holiday House, 1990.

☐ Leedy, Loreen. *Look at My Book: How Kids Can Write & Illustrate Terrific Books.* Holiday House, 2003.

☐ Leedy, Loreen. *Messages in the Mailbox: How to Write a Letter.* Holiday House, 1994.

☐ Leedy, Loreen. *There's a Frog in My Throat: 440 Animal Sayings a Little Bird Told Me.* Holiday House, 2003.

☐ Lichtenheld, Tom. *E-mergency!.* Chronicle Books, 2011.

☐ Maizels Jennie. *The Amazing Pop-up Grammar Book.* Dutton Juvenile, 1996.

☐ Petty Kate. *The Perfect Pop-Up Punctuation Book.* Dutton Juvenile, 2006.

☐ Pulver, Robin. *Silent Letters Loud and Clear.* Holiday House, 2010.

☐ Pulver, Robin. *Nouns and Verbs Have a Field Day.* Holiday House, 2007.

☐ Pulver, Robin. *Punctuation Takes a Vacation.* Holiday House, 2004.

☐ Pulver, Robin. *Happy Endings: A Story About Suffixes.* Holiday House, 2011.

☐ Truss. *Eats, Shoots & Leaves: Why, Commas Really Do Make a Difference!.* Putnam Juvenile, 2006.

☐ Truss. *The Girl's Like Spaghetti: Why, You Can't Manage without Apostrophes!.* Putnam Juvenile, 2007.

☐ Truss. *Twenty-Odd Ducks: Why, every punctuation mark counts!.* Putnam Juvenile, 2008.

☐ Turner, Priscilla. *The War Between the Vowels and the Consonants.* Farrar, Straus and Giroux, 1999.

☐ Walker, Sally M. *The Vowel Family: A Tale of Lost Letters.* Carolrhoda Books, 2008.

Series of Grammar Books (4th-8th Grades)

Words are Categorical

- [ ] Cleary, Brian P. *But and For, Yet and Nor: What is a Conjunction? (Words are Categorical)*. Carolrhoda, 2012.

- [ ] Cleary, Brian P. *Breezier, Cheesier, Newest, and Bluest: What Are Comparatives and Superlatives? (Words Are Categorical)*. Carolrhoda, 2013.

- [ ] Cleary, Brian P. *Cool! Whoa! Ah and Oh!: What Is an Interjection? (Words Are Categorical)*. Carolrhoda, 2013.

- [ ] Cleary, Brian P. *Dearly, Nearly, Insincerely: What Is An Adverb? (Words Are Categorical)*. Carolrhoda, 2005.

- [ ] Cleary, Brian P. *Feet and Puppies, Thieves and Guppies: What Are Irregular Plurals? (Words Are Categorical)*. Carolrhoda, 2012.

- [ ] Cleary, Brian P. *Hairy, Scary, Ordinary: What Is an Adjective? (Words Are Categorical)*. Carolrhoda, 2001.

- [ ] Cleary, Brian P. *How Much Can a Bare Bear Bear?: What Are Homonyms and Homophones? (Words Are Categorical)*. Carolrhoda, 2007.

- [ ] Cleary, Brian P. *I And You And Don't Forget Who: What Is a Pronoun? (Words Are Categorical)*. Carolrhoda, 2006.

- [ ] Cleary, Brian P. *I'm and Won't, They're and Don't: What's a Contraction? (Words Are Categorical)*. Carolrhoda, 2012.

- [ ] Cleary, Brian P. *Lazily, Crazily, Just a Bit Nasally: More About Adverbs (Words are Categorical)*. Carolrhoda, 2010.

- [ ] Cleary, Brian P. *A Lime, a Mime, a Pool of Slime: More About Nouns (Words Are Categorical)*. Carolrhoda, 2008.

- [ ] Cleary, Brian P. *Madam and Nun and 1001: What Is a Palindrome? (Words Are Categorical)*. Carolrhoda, 2012.

- [ ] Cleary, Brian P. *A Mink, a Fink, a Skating Rink: What Is a Noun? (Words Are Categorical)*. Carolrhoda, 1999.

- [ ] Cleary, Brian P. *Pitch and Throw, Grasp and Know: What Is a Synonym? (Words Are Categorical)*. Carolrhoda, 2007.

☐ Cleary, Brian P. *Quirky, Jerky, Extra Perky: More About Adjectives (Words Are Categorical)*. Carolrhoda, 2009.

☐ Cleary, Brian P. *Skin Like Milk, Hair of Silk: What Are Similes and Metaphors? (Words Are Categorical)*. Carolrhoda, 2011.

☐ Cleary, Brian P. *Slide and Slurp, Scratch and Burp: More About Verbs (Words Are Categorical)*. Carolrhoda, 2009.

☐ Cleary, Brian P. *Stop and Go, Yes and No: What Is an Antonym? (Words Are Categorical)*. Carolrhoda, 2008.

☐ Cleary, Brian P. *Straight and Curvy, Meek and Nervy: More About Antonyms (Words Are Categorical)*. Carolrhoda, 2011.

☐ Cleary, Brian P. *Stroll and Walk, Babble and Talk: More About Synonyms (Words Are Categorical)*. Carolrhoda, 2010.

☐ Cleary, Brian P. *Thumbtacks, Earwax, Lipstick, Dipstick: What Is a Compound Word? (Words Are Categorical)*. Carolrhoda, 2011.

☐ Cleary, Brian P. *To Root to Toot to Parachute: What Is a Verb (Words Are Categorical)*. Carolrhoda, 2001.

☐ Cleary, Brian P. *Under, Over, by the Clover: What Is a Preposition? (Words Are Categorical)*. Carolrhoda, 2003.

Rick Walton Books

☐ Walton, Rick. *Around the House the Fox Chased the Mouse: Adventures in Prepositions (Language Adventures Book)*. Gibbs Smith, 2011.

☐ Walton, Rick. *Bullfrog Pops!: Adventures in Verbs and Direct Objects (Language Adventures Book)*. Gibbs Smith, 2011.

☐ Walton, Rick. *Herd of Cows, Flock of Sheep: Adventures in Collective Nouns (Language Adventures Book)*. Gibbs Smith, 2011.

☐ Walton, Rick. *Just Me & 6,000 Rats: A Tale of Conjunctions (Language Adventures Book)*. Gibbs Smith, 2011.

☐ Walton, Rick. *Once There Was A Bull...(frog): Adventures in Compound Words (Language Adventures Book)*. Gibbs Smith, 2011.

☐ Walton, Rick. *Pig, Pigger, Piggest: Adventures in Comparing*. Gibbs Smith, 2011.

- ☐ Walton, Rick. *Suddenly Alligator: Adventures in Adverbs*. Gibbs Smith, 2011.
- ☐ Walton, Rick. *Why the Banana Split: Adventures in Idioms (Language Adventures Book)*. Gibbs Smith, 2011.

World of Language

- ☐ Heller, Ruth. *Behind the Mask: A Book about Prepositions (World of Language)*. Puffin, 1998.
- ☐ Heller, Ruth. *A Cache of Jewels (World of Language)*. Puffin, 1998.
- ☐ Heller, Ruth. *Fantastic! Wow! and Unreal!: A Book About Interjections and Conjunctions (World of Language)*. Puffin, 2000.
- ☐ Heller, Ruth. *Kites Sail High (World of Language)*. Puffin, 1998.
- ☐ Heller, Ruth. *Many Luscious Lollipops (World of Language)*. Puffin, 1998.
- ☐ Heller, Ruth. *Merry-Go-Round (World of Language)*. Puffin, 1998.
- ☐ Heller, Ruth. *Mine, All Mine! (World of Language)*. Puffin, 1999.
- ☐ Heller, Ruth. *Up, Up and Away (World of Language)*. Puffin, 1998.

Marvin Terban Books

- ☐ Terban, Marvin. *The Dove Dove: Funny Homograph Riddles*. Sandpiper, 2008.
- ☐ Terban, Marvin. *Eight Ate: A Feast of Homonym Riddles*. Sandpiper, 2007.
- ☐ Terban, Marvin. *Guppies in Tuxedos: Funny Eponyms*. Sandpiper, 2008.
- ☐ Terban, Marvin. *In a Pickle: And Other Funny Idioms*. Sandpiper, 2007.
- ☐ Terban, Marvin. *It Figures!: Fun Figures of Speech*. Sandpiper, 1993.
- ☐ Terban, Marvin. *Mad as a Wet Hen!: And Other Funny Idioms*. Sandpiper, 2007.
- ☐ Terban, Marvin. *Punching the Clock: Funny Action Idioms*. Sandpiper, 1990.
- ☐ Terban, Marvin. *Too Hot to Hoot: Funny Palindrome Riddles*. Sandpiper, 2008.
- ☐ Terban, Marvin. *Your Foot's on My Feet!: And Other Tricky Nouns*. Sandpiper, 2008.

Writing Games (4th-8th Grades)

- ☐ *McNeill Designs You've Been Sentenced: Brain-Buster Word Challenge Add-on Deck.* McNeil Designs. ASIN: 0641843267
- ☐ *McNeill Designs You've Been Sentenced: Gourmet Cuisine Add-on Deck.* McNeil Designs. ASIN: 0641843216
- ☐ *McNeill Designs You've Been Sentenced: NASA Space Terminology Add-on Deck.* McNeil Designs. ASIN: 1450751210
- ☐ *McNeill Designs You've Been Sentenced: Pop Culture Add-on Deck.* McNeil Designs. ASIN: 0641843208
- ☐ *McNeill Designs You've Been Sentenced: Sci-fi/Fantasy Add-on Deck.* McNeil Designs. ASIN: 0641843224
- ☐ *McNeill Designs You've Been Sentenced: Sports Highlights Add-on Deck.* McNeil Designs. ASIN: 0641843232
- ☐ *Rory's Story Cubes: Actions.* Gamewright. ASIN: B0063NC3N0
- ☐ *Rory's Story Cubes: Voyages.* Gamewright. ASIN: B009ZNJZV8
- ☐ *Speedeebee.* Blue Orange. ASIN: B007JPS3LC
- ☐ *Synonyms: The Word Game That Gets Your Mind Racing.* Lindergaff, LLC. ASIN: B004G7B3NQ
- ☐ *Tell Tale.* Blue Orange. ASIN: B004P13H5U
- ☐ *Tell Tale Fairy Tales.* Blue Orange. ASIN: B007JPS3NK
- ☐ *You've Been Sentenced.* McNeil Designs. ASIN: B000EVLZ9U

Real Art History Books

Art History Books for K-3rd Grades

General Art History Books (K-3rd Grades)

- ☐ Arrigan, Mary. *Mario's Angels: A Story About the Artist Giotto.*
- ☐ Blaisdell, Molly. *Rembrandt and the Boy Who Drew Dogs: A story about Rembrandt van Rijn.*
- ☐ Bryant, Jen. *A Splash of Red: The Life and Art of Horace Pippin.*
- ☐ Capatti, Berenice. *Klimt and His Cat.*
- ☐ Comora, Madeleine. *Rembrandt and Titus: Artist and Son.*
- ☐ De Brunhoff, Laurent. *Babar's Museum of Art.*
- ☐ Greenberg, Jan. *Action Jackson.*
- ☐ Guarnieri, Paolo. *A Boy Named Giotto.*
- ☐ Hong, Chen Jiang. *The Magic Horse of Han Gan.*
- ☐ Hooper, Meredith. *Celebrity Cat: With Paintings from Art Galleries Around the World.*
- ☐ Hooper, Meredith. *Dogs' Night.*
- ☐ Johnson, D.B. *Magritte's Marvelous Hat.*
- ☐ Obiolis, Anna. *Dali and the Path of Dreams.*
- ☐ Rodriguez, Rachel Victoria. *Building on Nature: The Life of Antoni Gaudi.*
- ☐ Rubin, Susan Goldman. *The Yellow House: Vincent Van Gogh and Paul Gauguin Side by Side.*
- ☐ Smith Jr., Charles. *Brick by Brick.* Building the White House
- ☐ Spiotta-DiMare, Loren. *Rockwell: A Boy and His Dog.*
- ☐ Stone, Tanya Lee. *Sandy's Circus: A Story About Alexander Calder.*
- ☐ Sweeney, Joan. *Bijou, Bonbon and Beau: The Kittens Who Danced for Degas.*
- ☐ Sweeney, Joan. *Suzette and the Puppy: A Story About Mary Cassatt.*
- ☐ Warhola, James. *Uncle Andy's.*

- [ ] Warhola, James. *Uncle Andy's Cats.*
- [ ] Winter, Jeannette. *My Name is Georgia.*
- [ ] Winter, Jonah. *Frida.*
- [ ] Winter, Jonah. *Just Behave, Pablo Picasso!*

Series of Art History Books (K-3rd Grades)

Katie and the Artists

- [ ] Mayhew, James. *Katie and the Bathers.*
- [ ] Mayhew, James. *Katie and the British Artists.*
- [ ] Mayhew, James. *Katie and the Mona Lisa.*
- [ ] Mayhew, James. *Katie and the Spanish Princess.*
- [ ] Mayhew, James. *Katie and the Starry Night.*
- [ ] Mayhew, James. *Katie and the Sunflowers.*
- [ ] Mayhew, James. *Katie and the Waterlily Pond: A Magical Journey Through Five Monet Masterpieces.*
- [ ] Mayhew, James. *Katie Meets The Impressionists.*
- [ ] Mayhew, James. *Katie's Picture Show.*
- [ ] Mayhew, James. *Katie's Sunday Afternoon.*

Anholt's Artists

- [ ] Anholt, Laurence. *Cezanne and the Apple Boy (Anholt's Artists).*
- [ ] Anholt, Laurence. *Degas and the Little Dancer (Anholt's Artists).*
- [ ] Anholt, Laurence. *Leonardo and the Flying Boy (Anholt's Artists).*
- [ ] Anholt, Laurence. *Matisse the King of Color (Anholt's Artists).*
- [ ] Anholt, Laurence. *Picasso and the Girl with a Ponytail (Anholt's Artists).*
- [ ] Anholt, Laurence. *Renoir and the Boy with the Long Hair (Anholt's Artists).*
- [ ] Anholt, Laurence. *The Magical Garden of Claude Monet (Anholt's Artists).*
- [ ] Anholt, Laurence. *Van Gogh and the Sunflowers (Anholt's Artists).*

Art History Books for 4th-8th Grades

General Art History Books (4th-8th Grades)

- ☐ Balliett, Blue. *Chasing Vermeer.*
- ☐ Balliett, Blue. *The Wright Three.*
- ☐ Balliett, Blue. *The Calder Game.*
- ☐ Bryant, Jen. *A Splash of Red: The Life and Art of Horace Pippin.*
- ☐ Denzel, Justen. *The Boy of the Painted Cave.*
- ☐ De Trevino, Elizabeth Borton. *I, Juan de Pareja.*
- ☐ Draeger, Kristin J. *Mona Lisa: Art History Disguised as Fun*
- ☐ Greenberg, Jan. *Action Jackson.*
- ☐ Greenberg, Jan. *Vincent Van Gogh: Portrait of an Artist.*
- ☐ Guarnieri, Paolo. *A Boy Named Giotto.*
- ☐ Hong, Chen Jiang. *The Magic Horse of Han Gan.*
- ☐ Konigsburg, E.L. *The Second Mrs. Gioconda.*
- ☐ Obiolis, Anna. *Dali and the Path of Dreams.*
- ☐ Oneal, Zibby. *Grandma Moses: Painter of Rural America.*
- ☐ Place, Francois. *The Old Man Mad About Drawing: A Tale of Hokusai.*
- ☐ Ray, Deborah Kogan. *Hokusai: The Man Who Painted a Mountain.*
- ☐ Shafer, Anders C. *The Fantastic Journey of Pieter Bruegel.*
- ☐ Smith Jr., Charles. *Brick by Brick.* Building the White House
- ☐ Spiotta-DiMare, Loren. *Rockwell: A Boy and His Dog.*
- ☐ Stanley, Diane. *Michelangelo.*
- ☐ Van Leeuwen, Jean. *The Great Googlestein Museum Mystery.*
- ☐ Warhola, James. *Uncle Andy's.*
- ☐ Warhola, James. *Uncle Andy's Cats.*
- ☐ Winter, Jeannette. *My Name is Georgia.*
- ☐ Winter, Jonah. *Frida.*

Series of Art History Books (4th-8th Grades)

Getting to Know the World's Greatest Artists

☐ Venezia, Mike. *Alexander Calder (Getting to Know the World's Greatest Artists).*

☐ Venezia, Mike. *Andy Warhol (Getting to Know the World's Greatest Artists).*

☐ Venezia, Mike. *Botticelli (Getting to Know the World's Greatest Artists).*

☐ Venezia, Mike. *Camille Pissarro (Getting to Know the World's Greatest Artists).*

☐ Venezia, Mike. *Da Vinci (Getting to Know the World's Greatest Artists).*

☐ Venezia, Mike. *Diego de Velazquez (Getting to Know the World's Greatest Artists).*

☐ Venezia, Mike. *Diego Rivera (Getting to Know the World's Greatest Artists).*

☐ Venezia, Mike. *Dorthea Lange (Getting to Know the World's Greatest Artists).*

☐ Venezia, Mike. *Edgar Degas (Getting to Know the World's Greatest Artists).*

☐ Venezia, Mike. *Edward Hopper (Getting to Know the World's Greatest Artists).*

☐ Venezia, Mike. *El Greco (Getting to Know the World's Greatest Artists).*

☐ Venezia, Mike. *Eugene Delacroix (Getting to Know the World's Greatest Artists).*

☐ Venezia, Mike. *Faith Ringgold (Getting to Know the World's Greatest Artists).*

☐ Venezia, Mike. *Francisco Goya (Getting to Know the World's Greatest Artists).*

☐ Venezia, Mike. *Frederic Remington (Getting to Know the World's Greatest Artists).*

☐ Venezia, Mike. *Frida Kahlo (Getting to Know the World's Greatest Artists).*

☐ Venezia, Mike. *Georges Seurat (Getting to Know the World's Greatest Artists).*

☐ Venezia, Mike. *Georgia O'Keeffe (Getting to Know the World's Greatest Artists).*

☐ Venezia, Mike. *Giotto (Getting to Know the World's Greatest Artists).*

☐ Venezia, Mike. *Grandma Moses (Getting to Know the World's Greatest Artists).*

☐ Venezia, Mike. *Grant Wood (Getting to Know the World's Greatest Artists).*

☐ Venezia, Mike. *Henri de toulouse-Lautrec (Getting to Know the World's Greatest Artists).*

☐ Venezia, Mike. *Henri Matisse (Getting to Know the World's Greatest Artists).*

☐ Venezia, Mike. *Henri Rousseau (Getting to Know the World's Greatest Artists).*

☐ Venezia, Mike. *Horace Pippin (Getting to Know the World's Greatest Artists).*

☐ Venezia, Mike. *Jackson Pollock (Getting to Know the World's Greatest Artists).*

☐ Venezia, Mike. *Jacob Lawrence (Getting to Know the World's Greatest Artists).*

☐ Venezia, Mike. *James McNeill Whistler (Getting to Know the World's Greatest Artists).*

- ☐ Venezia, Mike. *Johannes Vermeer (Getting to Know the World's Greatest Artists)*.
- ☐ Venezia, Mike. *Marc Chagall (Getting to Know the World's Greatest Artists)*.
- ☐ Venezia, Mike. *Mary Cassatt (Getting to Know the World's Greatest Artists)*.
- ☐ Venezia, Mike. *Michelangelo (Getting to Know the World's Greatest Artists)*.
- ☐ Venezia, Mike. *Monet (Getting to Know the World's Greatest Artists)*.
- ☐ Venezia, Mike. *Norman Rockwell (Getting to Know the World's Greatest Artists)*.
- ☐ Venezia, Mike. *Paul Cezanne (Getting to Know the World's Greatest Artists)*.
- ☐ Venezia, Mike. *Paul Gauguin (Getting to Know the World's Greatest Artists)*.
- ☐ Venezia, Mike. *Paul Klee (Getting to Know the World's Greatest Artists)*.
- ☐ Venezia, Mike. *Peter Bruegel (Getting to Know the World's Greatest Artists)*.
- ☐ Venezia, Mike. *Picasso (Getting to Know the World's Greatest Artists)*.
- ☐ Venezia, Mike. *Pierre Auguste Renoir (Getting to Know the World's Greatest Artists)*.
- ☐ Venezia, Mike. *Raphael (Getting to Know the World's Greatest Artists)*.
- ☐ Venezia, Mike. *Rembrandt (Getting to Know the World's Greatest Artists)*.
- ☐ Venezia, Mike. *René Magritte (Getting to Know the World's Greatest Artists)*.
- ☐ Venezia, Mike. *Roy Lichtenstein (Getting to Know the World's Greatest Artists)*.
- ☐ Venezia, Mike. *Salvador Dali (Getting to Know the World's Greatest Artists)*.
- ☐ Venezia, Mike. *Titian (Getting to Know the World's Greatest Artists)*.
- ☐ Venezia, Mike. *Van Gogh (Getting to Know the World's Greatest Artists)*.
- ☐ Venezia, Mike. *Winslow Homer (Getting to Know the World's Greatest Artists)*.

Art History Disguised as Fun

- ☐ Draeger, Kristin J. *American Art History: Volume I*
- ☐ Draeger, Kristin J. *American Art History: Volume II*
- ☐ Draeger, Kristin J. *Drawing American Art: Volume I*
- ☐ Draeger, Kristin J. *Drawing American Art: Volume II*

Made in the USA
San Bernardino, CA
31 December 2017